The Invisible Manager

How AI Empowers Project Managers to Work Smarter, Not Harder
Reduce your workload by atleast 50%

Ajay Tiwari

qurate
quratebooks.com

THE INVISIBLE MANAGER
Ajay Tiwari

Published in 2025

© Published by

Qurate Books Pvt. Ltd.
Goa 403523, India
www.quratebooks.com
Tel: 1800-210-6527, Email: info@quratebooks.com

ISBN: 978-93-58982-17-6

Dedicated To

The Project Managers who embrace challenges with courage,
The Innovators who see possibilities where others see limitations,
and to every curious mind daring to chart new frontiers,
this book is for you.
May it inspire you to harness the power of technology and wisdom,
to lead with heart and strategy,
and to redefine what's possible.
Here's to your journey of growth, discovery and excellence.

Preface

The world of project management is undergoing a seismic shift. What was once a discipline rooted in spreadsheets, Gantt charts, and team meetings is now evolving into something far more dynamic, intuitive, and efficient. Artificial Intelligence (AI) is no longer a futuristic concept, it is here, transforming how we think, work, and lead. Yet, amidst this transformation, project managers find themselves standing at a crossroads: How do we navigate this new landscape? How do we harness the power of AI without losing the human touch that makes great leadership possible?

This book, *The Invisible Manager: How AI Empowers Project Managers to Work Smarter, Not Harder,* was born from my own journey through these questions. It is a journey that began with skepticism and uncertainty but blossomed into a deep understanding of AI as a powerful ally -a silent partner that enhances our capabilities, sharpens our decision-making, and liberates us from the tyranny of repetitive tasks.

In the pages that follow, you will step into the shoes of Arjun, a project manager navigating the challenges of complex projects in a rapidly evolving world. Through his experiences, you will see AI not as a threat to traditional project management but as a bridge to its future. Each chapter is designed to demystify AI, offering you practical insights, actionable strategies, and a vision for what's possible when technology and human intuition come together.

This is not a technical manual. It's a guide, a companion for project managers who are curious about the possibilities AI offers and who want to embark on their own journey of transformation. Whether you're managing embedded systems, aerospace projects, or multidisciplinary teams, the lessons in this book are universal. They're about embracing change, fostering collaboration, and growing alongside the tools we create.

As you turn the pages, I hope you'll find inspiration, empowerment, and a renewed sense of curiosity. The future of project management is bright, and it's waiting for leaders like you to shape it.

Why should learning project management be boring?

Welcome to the journey!

- Ajay Tiwari
Program Manager
PMP, PSM 2, PSPO 2, Agile Practitioner, specialist in handling complex projects with new technologies

***

Introduction

Project management has always been a balancing act—juggling cost, scope, time, resources, and quality while keeping an eye on the ever-elusive goal of stakeholder satisfaction. In my career, I've witnessed the evolution of project management methodologies, from the rigid structures of waterfall to the agile dynamism of Scrum and Kanban. Yet, none of these shifts compares to the transformative potential of artificial intelligence.

AI has the power to fundamentally reshape how we approach our work. It doesn't just automate—it augments. It doesn't just execute—it anticipates. For project managers, this means more than efficiency; it means empowerment. It means stepping into a role where strategic thinking and human empathy take center stage, supported by a technological partner that handles the rest.

This is not just another book about technology or tools—it's a narrative. Through Arjun's journey, I have tried to masterfully weave together the theoretical and the practical, the aspirational and the actionable. Each chapter unfolds like a story, inviting readers to not just learn about AI but to see themselves using it, thriving with it, and growing because of it.

What sets this book apart is its humanity. While it celebrates AI's capabilities, it never loses sight of the human element—the creativity, judgment, and leadership that only we can bring. It recognizes that AI is not a replacement for project managers but a **catalyst** for their evolution.

As you read *The Invisible Manager,* you'll find yourself equipped not only with tools and techniques but also with a mindset—a growth mindset that will enable you to navigate the challenges and opportunities of an AI-driven world. This book is an invitation to reimagine what's possible, to embrace the invisible ally at your side, and to lead with confidence into the next frontier of project management. It's an exciting time to be a project manager. With AI, the future is not something to fear—it's something to build.

***

About the Author

Ajay Tiwari is an experienced program manager, technologist, and thought leader passionate about transforming the way we work. With over 15 years of experience managing complex projects across industries such as aerospace, automotive, biomedical, industrial, AI, cybersecurity, Ajay Tiwari has seen firsthand the challenges project managers face in balancing technology, people, processes, and priorities.

In recent years, Ajay Tiwari has dedicated his career to exploring how artificial intelligence can empower project managers, turning their toughest challenges into opportunities for growth and innovation. He is known for his practical, approachable insights into AI and their ability to bridge the gap between technical knowledge and real-world application.

When Ajay Tiwari isn't writing or working, he can be found mentoring aspiring project managers, working with team, experimenting with new AI tools, or spending time with his family.

This book is a culmination of his journey, an invitation for project managers to step confidently into the future and embrace AI as their greatest ally.

***

Contents

Which Type of Manager Are You?

Project management is a multifaceted field that caters to professionals at various stages of their careers. Understanding the roles within project management helps individuals identify where they stand and how they can grow. Here's a breakdown of the common types of managers in the world, along with guidance on why they should read this book:

1. **Project Assistant/Coordinator**
    - **Role:** Works closely with the Project Manager and the team to handle administrative and operational tasks, ensuring smooth project progression.
    - **Example:** Anil, a Project Coordinator, tracks the progress of a marketing campaign, schedules team meetings, and ensures all documentation is up to date.

Why Should You Read: This book is a great resource for coordinators aiming to understand higher-level project management processes and transition into a Project Manager role.

2. **Project Manager**
   - **Role:** Plans, executes, monitors, and closes individual projects while focusing on scope, budget, timeline, and quality. Specialized roles like Technical Project Managers combine domain knowledge with traditional project management.
   - **Example:** Balaji, a Technical Project Manager in a software company, ensures a mobile app launch meets user requirements while staying on schedule and within budget.
   - **Why Should You Read:** Essential for Project Managers looking to leverage AI, streamline processes, and enhance their decision-making skills.
3. **Program Manager**
   - **Role:** Oversees multiple related projects to ensure they align with organizational goals and deliver integrated benefits.
   - **Example:** Catherine manages a digital transformation program, ensuring projects like cloud migration, process automation, and employee training are interlinked and deliver value together.
   - **Why Should You Read:** Perfect for Program Managers who want to master advanced AI tools for managing complexity and ensuring alignment with strategic goals.
4. **Portfolio Manager**
   - **Role:** Manages a collection of programs and projects, focusing on alignment with strategic objectives and balancing priorities.
   - **Example:** Danny oversees an IT portfolio, deciding which projects should be funded based on ROI and risk analysis.

- **Why Should You Read:** Suitable for Portfolio Managers seeking frameworks to integrate AI in strategic planning and resource allocation.

5. **Product Manager**
   - **Role:** Guides the development and lifecycle of a product, ensuring alignment with customer needs, business goals, and market demands. Acts as a bridge between teams like engineering, marketing, and sales.
   - **Example:** Eela, a Product Manager for an e-commerce platform, collaborates with developers and marketers to launch a new feature that boosts customer retention.
   - **Why Should You Read:** Ideal for Product Managers eager to explore AI-driven customer insights, product roadmapping, and market analysis.
6. **PMO Manager**
   - **Role:** Leads the Project Management Office, standardizing processes, methodologies, and tools across all projects and programs.
   - **Example:** Franco, a PMO Manager, implements organization-wide project dashboards to ensure consistency and transparency in reporting.
   - **Why Should You Read:** Best for PMO Managers who want to integrate AI to drive standardization and optimize team performance.

Preparing for the Journey

Before diving into advanced project management techniques, it's essential to grasp the basics. This book assumes familiarity with the foundational principles outlined in PMBOK 6 and 7. If you're new to these frameworks, a brief review will ensure you maximize the value of this guide.

This book is your companion for evolving in your project management career, whether you're a beginner stepping into coordination or a seasoned professional navigating strategic portfolios. Let's explore how AI can empower your journey!

If you are new to project management you may visit my website: https://theinvisiblemanager.com/

***

The Invisible Ally

"Change is the law of life. And those who look only to the past or present are certain to miss the future."

– John F. Kennedy

Arjun's Growing Frustration

Arjun was sitting in his office, staring at the screen in front of him, his fingers tapping restlessly on the desk. The coffee on his table had long gone cold, but he barely noticed. His thoughts were consumed by the mess of his current project. The product launch is just a few weeks away, but everything seems to be falling apart. The design team was behind schedule, the marketing department was raising alarms, and the budget had exceeded expectations. No matter how many times he went over the spreadsheets or adjusted the timelines, nothing seemed to stick. The pressure was mounting as his reputation was on the line.

He knew this feeling all too well. The crushing weight of responsibility pressed down on his shoulders, and he felt pulled in a thousand different directions, each demand louder than the last. But this time, it wasn't just stress. It was something deeper. The project felt like it was slipping away, unraveling despite his efforts. No matter how hard he tried to hold it together, it kept falling apart, like sand slipping through his fingers.

He was lost in the details, overwhelmed by spreadsheets, timelines, and a constant stream of emails. His clarity was gone, replaced by a fog of confusion and exhaustion. Just as he leaned forward to tackle yet another wave of data, his phone buzzed sharply. The sound broke the silence like a snap, pulling him abruptly back into the moment

It was a message from Krishna.

"Hey, Arjun! Have you ever thought about using AI tools to help manage your projects? I've been using them, and they're a game-changer. Let's chat soon."

Arjun stared at the message. AI? I have heard of it, of course. Everyone has. But AI in project management? The idea seems absurd. Wasn't AI something to be used for answering questions, automating chatbots or use in self-driving cars, and not managing a multi-million-dollar product launch?

But Krishna was no stranger to innovative ideas. If there was anyone who could pull off something like this, it would be him. Arjun hesitated but eventually replied, "Okay, let's talk later. Maybe you can show me what you mean."

Later that afternoon, they met in the office lounge. Krishna's usual calm demeanor was unchanged, as if the world outside was nothing but a backdrop to his cool unwavering confidence.

"I know you're probably skeptical," Krishna began, flashing Arjun one of his knowing smiles. "But let me show you something that might just change everything."

Arjun wasn't sure what to expect. "I don't know, Krishna. I've got enough on my plate right now. The last thing I need is some new tool that'll add more confusion." Krishna's smile widened. "I promise, it won't add confusion. It'll clear it up."

He pulled out a device, and before Arjun could say anything else, Krishna was already asking questions. The hologram flickered for a moment before loading a sleek interface, a dashboard filled with colorful graphs, timelines, and tasks that looked almost too good to be true.

"This," Krishna said with a flourish, "is your new best friend!"

Arjun leaned in, unsure whether to be impressed or skeptical. "What is it? A new project management software?"

Krishna shook his head. "It's not just software. It's an AI-powered tool. It learns. It adapts. It gives you insights that you would never get by yourself." Arjun's eyebrows furrowed. "AI? Like... what, a robot project manager?"

Krishna laughed. "Not exactly. Think of it more like an invisible ally who's always working behind the scenes, analyzing data, making predictions, and giving you recommendations based on patterns it recognizes. It doesn't replace you. It amplifies you."

Arjun was intrigued, though still cautious. "Okay, so how does it work?"

Krishna didn't answer immediately. Instead, he began to ask questions again, feeding a few details about Arjun's current project. A few seconds later, the AI began to process the information, and the hologram lit up with suggestions.

"This is where the magic happens," Krishna said quietly, watching Arjun's face.

"See here?" Krishna pointed to a graph showing the project's budget and timeline. "The AI just identified that if you keep going with the current resource allocation, your project will exceed the budget by 37%. But here's the interesting part, it suggests reassigning a couple of developers from a different project to help with design, which will bring everything back on track."

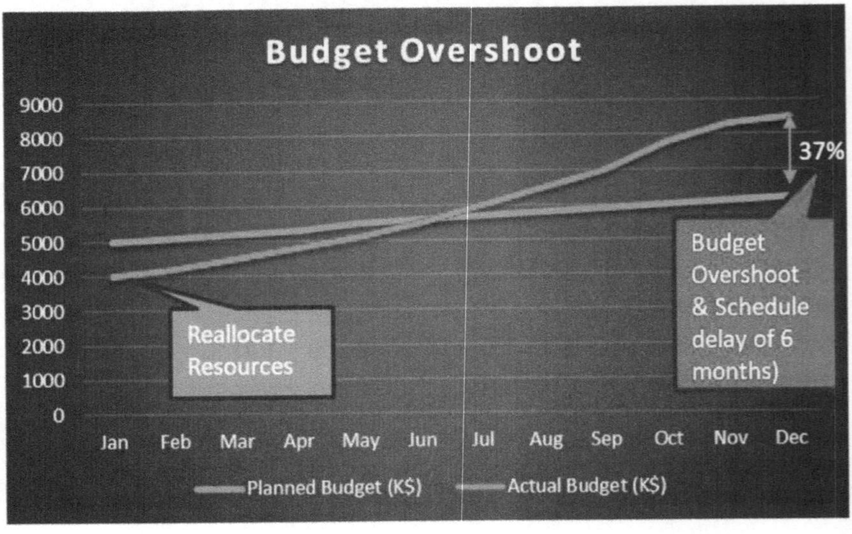

Arjun stared at the display, his curiosity piqued. "Wait a minute. It's telling me to reassign people? How does it know that?"

Krishna's grin widened. "It knows because it's not just about the project you're working on right now. It analyzes your entire portfolio, past projects, team performance, resource utilization, even external factors like market trends. It can predict where things are going wrong before you even realize it."

Arjun blinked. "This... this is insane. How can a machine understand all that?"

Krishna's expression grew serious. "Because AI isn't just a tool. It's a partner. It learns patterns, draws from thousands of data points, and gives you insights that can make or break your project."

The next day, Arjun decided to give it a try. His project was at a critical point, and despite his hesitation, he couldn't afford to ignore any possible solution. He uploaded the project data into the AI tool, half-expecting it to be another gimmick. He waited, tapping his foot impatiently as the AI crunched the numbers. Moments later, the tool suggested some adjustments to the team structure, proposed new timelines, and even highlighted a hidden risk: a potential bottleneck in the marketing approval process that Arjun hadn't noticed. The AI tool's recommendations felt almost too perfect—too spot-on.

Arjun frowned, his skepticism still intact. "Alright, I'll make some of these changes, but I'm double-checking everything myself."

But as the days passed, something unexpected happened. The project started to move faster. The development team, which had been falling behind, caught up. The marketing team, once slow to approve assets, moved swiftly through the process. And most importantly, the AI's prediction about the bottleneck proved true. The tool had flagged a miscommunication between marketing and design, something Arjun had completely missed in his rush to manage the bigger tasks.

By the time the product was ready for launch, Arjun felt something he hadn't experienced in weeks: relief. The project was on time, on budget, and the team was functioning better than ever.

Krishna's words echoed in Arjun's mind as he sat back in his chair, looking at the final report. "The AI doesn't replace you. It amplifies you." It was true. The AI had been there every step of the way, pointing out risks, suggesting solutions, and allowing Arjun to make better, faster decisions. He hadn't needed to micromanage every detail. The AI had taken care of that, leaving Arjun free to focus on the human side of leadership: motivation, communication, and decision-making.

Arjun's transformation didn't end with the successful project launch. It had sparked a curiosity in him. What else could AI do for his work? What other mysteries could it unravel, what other opportunities could it reveal? The truth was clear now: AI wasn't the future of project management. It was the present. And it was the invisible ally every project manager needed, quietly working in the background to turn chaos into order, stress into success.

The Invisible Ally

As Arjun was pondering on the Stacey Matrix image in front of his desk and got deeper in his thoughts, *I used the AI for complicated embedded project but is it good enough for the advanced chaotic projects such as autonomous driving or eVTOL in the Embedded too?. Lets figure it out, since the success of the previous project has given me a recognition and management is going to provide a challenging project to me.*

Arjun leaned back in his chair, his gaze fixed on the Stacey Matrix pinned on the corkboard above his desk. The top right label "Chaotic" where the requirements & technology are still evolving & unknown, seemed to almost pulsate under the harsh fluorescent light of his workspace. His thoughts churned, caught between the thrill of what he had achieved and the uncertainty of what lay ahead.

He tapped his pen against the desk rhythmically, each tap resonating with the question looping in his mind: *AI had worked wonders for the complicated embedded project - its precision, its ability to forecast potential pitfalls, its quiet, invisible efficiency. But was it truly ready to face the maelstrom of chaos that defined advanced projects like autonomous driving or eVTOL systems?*

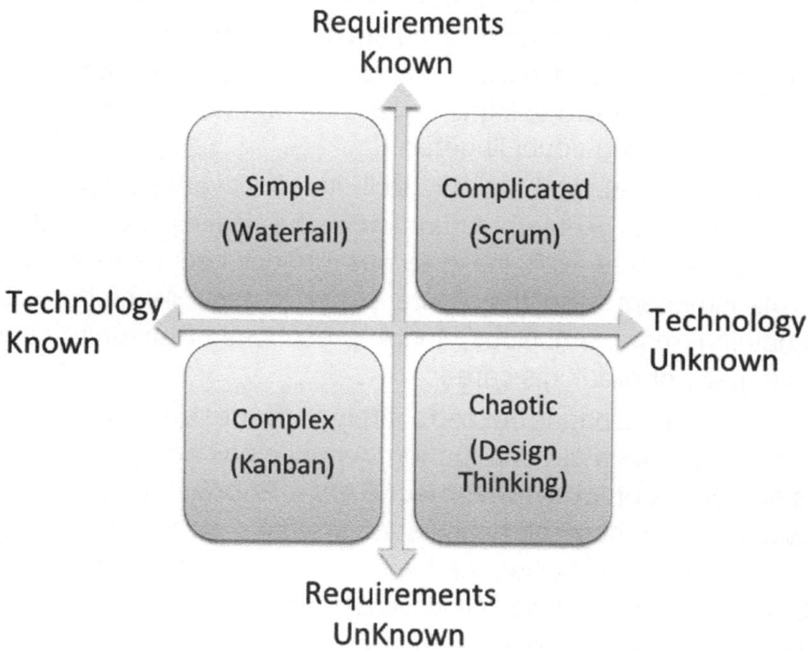

The Stacey Matrix was clear, these projects weren't just complex; they were chaotic. Variables changed not daily, but hourly. Dependencies were not just tangled, they were outright unpredictable. Decisions had to be made on the fly, and the cost of a single misstep could spiral into millions or worse, lives.

Arjun sat forward, the chair creaking under the shift of weight. His fingers hovered over the keyboard as he pulled up the project documentation for his previous AI-assisted success. The victory had been sweet, his approach had not only delivered results but had also earned him recognition. His name had been mentioned in meetings where executives usually skipped over the names of project managers. Yet, with recognition came expectation, and with expectation came a new challenge, one that he suspected was already en-route to his desk.

The thought both excited and unsettled him. *Could AI be my ally in the chaos of autonomous driving?* He wondered, pulling up industry case studies on how AI was being used in such projects. The data was compelling - predictive models that adjusted in real time, AI algorithms that could simulate millions of scenarios before finalizing a course of action, machine learning tools that could analyze and optimize designs faster than any team of engineers. But still, a nagging doubt lingered.

AI was a tool, and like any tool, its effectiveness depended on how it was wielded. Arjun knew the stakes were higher now. His success with the previous project had been noticed by management, and they were eager to test his mettle with something more ambitious, more precarious. Something that could make or break his career.

Just then, his phone buzzed sharply on the desk, slicing through his thoughts like a siren in the fog. A new email notification lit up the screen, **Subject: *New Project Brief – Priority Review***. Arjun hesitated for a moment, his cursor hovering over the email. This was it—the moment when the hypothetical would turn into reality. He clicked, and the screen filled with a document marked with bold headers: ***Level 5 Autonomous Driving System Development: Integration of Embedded AI for Real-Time Decision-Making.***

The complexity of the challenge hit him like a wave. This was no ordinary project. Autonomous driving wasn't just about programming cars to move from Point A to Point B. It was about creating systems that could think, adapt, and respond faster than a human in environments riddled with unpredictability. Every input from weather conditions to the unexpected behavior of other drivers had to be processed in milliseconds.

Arjun's heartbeat quickened as he scrolled through the brief. The project was massive, involving multiple teams, suppliers, and layers of regulation. Yet, amidst the enormity, his thoughts kept circling back to one thing: *How could AI help me not just survive this storm but conquer it?*

His eyes darted back to the Stacey Matrix. The chaotic zone didn't look intimidating anymore, it looked like an opportunity. "I've proven AI can handle complexity," he muttered to himself. "But chaos... chaos is a different beast altogether. Can AI evolve from being just a tool to becoming a true partner?"

His mind raced with possibilities. What if he could integrate AI not just for decision-making but for continuous learning throughout the project? Could AI systems predict supply chain disruptions before they happened? Could they simulate edge cases for autonomous driving scenarios no human could anticipate? And then, a more ambitious thought struck him: *What if the AI became the heartbeat of the project, driving innovation and efficiency at a pace humans alone could never achieve?*

A notification from his calendar popped up: **"Management Briefing: Tomorrow 9:00 AM."**

Arjun smiled wryly. The gauntlet had been thrown, and he had no intention of shying away. Standing, he grabbed a marker and began sketching on the whiteboard next to his desk. Ideas flowed as he mapped out how AI could be used to tackle every conceivable hurdle in the upcoming project. The room was quiet except for the faint hum of his laptop. He gazed at the messy whiteboard, the scribbles now forming the skeleton of a plan - a roadmap that merged human ingenuity with AI's unrelenting precision. "This is just the beginning," he said to himself, his voice filled with a mix of determination and curiosity. "Let's figure it out," he whispered. "This isn't just a challenge, it's a chance to redefine what's possible in embedded systems."

With that, he powered down his laptop, feeling the weight of what lay ahead. The success of the previous project had given him recognition, yes but now, it was time to prove that success was not a fluke. It was a foundation.

Tomorrow would mark the start of a journey not just into a new project, but into uncharted territory where the boundaries of

AI and human ingenuity would be tested like never before. Arjun wasn't just stepping into a new challenge; he was stepping into a new era.

And he wasn't going alone.

AI, as Arjun discovered, isn't just a tool - it's a silent partner, always learning, adapting, and providing insights that empower project managers to make smarter, faster decisions. Arjun had gone from being a skeptic to a believer, realizing that the right AI tools didn't replace the human touch, they enhanced it. In the fast-paced, ever-changing world of project management, having an invisible ally like AI is no longer a luxury - it's a necessity. And just like Arjun, once you experience its full potential, you'll wonder how you ever managed without it.

As Arjun now understood, AI doesn't make decisions for you—it makes the decision-making process smarter, faster, and more accurate. The invisible ally is here to stay.

The Invisible Ally: Your Next Step into AI-Enhanced Project Management

The story of Arjun's journey illustrates a critical turning point for project managers everywhere. It's no longer about if AI can assist in managing projects - it's about how effectively you can wield it as your invisible ally.

The question now is: **Are you ready to take the leap?**

Arjun moved from skepticism to belief, using AI tools to transform a struggling project into a resounding success. His newfound ally didn't replace his skills but amplified them, uncovering risks, optimizing resources, and helping him focus on leadership. As he faces a new challenge - venturing into the chaotic domain of autonomous systems - the role of AI is set to evolve further, becoming not just a tool but a true partner in navigating complexity.

AI is no longer just a tool, it's your partner in success, whether you're managing routine projects or tackling the unknown. It allows you to transition from micromanagement to strategic leadership, freeing your time to focus on the human aspects of project management.

Start small. Choose one tool. Test its potential. And let AI become your invisible ally in turning chaos into clarity and stress into success.

Are you ready to join Arjun on this journey? The tools are at your fingertips. Start exploring, experimenting, and excelling today!

RISE

Research: Explore AI tools relevant to your domain. Understand their capabilities and identify which ones address your project management needs.

Implement: Start with a single task or challenge. Use AI tools to automate, optimize, or analyze. Experiment with practical applications like planning timelines or predicting risks.

Strategize: Leverage AI insights to refine your approach. Use predictive analytics to anticipate challenges, optimize resources, and foster better collaboration.

Evaluate: Regularly assess the impact of AI on your workflow. Compare traditional methods with AI-enhanced processes to measure improvements and identify areas for growth.

Call to Action

If you're ready to unlock the potential of AI, here's how you can start:

1. Leverage AI Tools for Current Challenges

Begin with tools that can handle the day-to-day complexities of your projects. For example:

- **ChatGPT:** Whatever execution level you are in, ask relevant questions such as: If you are in planning stage ask, "What is the most effective way to structure this project timeline while accounting for unforeseen delays?"

- **Microsoft CoPilot:** Since majority of the companies have tied up with Microsoft you can leverage copilot instead of ChatGPT. This can be used even for coding as well.
- **Google Gemini:** Another AI tool for searching answer to relevant questions. Use multiple AI tools to get more insights on the problems being faced.
- Ask AI tools what kind of ***prompts*** to be asked as a project manager. Check **Appendix 1** for the different prompts. This should minimum reduce 30% of your work daily. I use it regularly for these activities including refining emails, generating ideas, research, risks and other process areas.

How to Use It: Start small, upload one project, experiment with AI suggestions, and observe the changes in efficiency and decision-making.

Follow the **template** in **Appendix 2** for capturing the task on how it was done traditionally and now with AI assistance what is the time reduction.

2. Elevate Decision-Making with Predictive Analytics

For larger and more complex projects, GENAI tools have to learn from previous projects and provide insights based on past performance and market trends. You can train one of the tools mentioned above with the past data:

- Automate projections for budgets and timelines.
- Identify hidden risks and anticipate roadblocks before they occur.
- Improve cross-team collaboration through AI-optimized workflows.

How to Use It: Integrate AI tools with your existing project management platforms. Train your team to interpret AI insights effectively to complement their expertise.

Appendix 1: ChatGPT/other prompts for Project Managers

Prompts for Planning and Strategy

1. "What is the most efficient way to structure this project timeline while accounting for unforeseen delays?"
2. "How can I ensure every team member understands the project's goals and their role in achieving them?"
3. "What innovative approaches can I use to break this complex problem into actionable tasks?"
4. "If I had to finish this project in half the time, what tasks or processes would I prioritize?"
5. "What potential risks am I overlooking, and how can I preemptively address them?"

Prompts for Communication and Collaboration

6. "What is the clearest way to explain this project update to stakeholders who aren't familiar with the technical details?"
7. "How can I motivate my team to stay engaged during a long or complex project?"
8. "What feedback mechanisms can I set up to ensure open communication across all levels of the project?"
9. "What is the best way to mediate a disagreement between team members over competing priorities?"
10. "How can I adapt my communication style to suit the needs of this particular audience?"

Prompts for Problem-Solving

11. "What are three creative solutions to this bottleneck, and which one aligns best with the project's goals?"
12. "How can I turn this unexpected challenge into an opportunity for improvement?"

13. "What lessons from past projects can I apply to solve this issue effectively?"
14. "What would a successful resolution of this problem look like, and what steps can I take to get there?"
15. "How can I use AI or automation tools to streamline this task or solve this problem?"

Prompts for Risk Management

16. "What are the top risks for this project, and how can I mitigate them effectively?"
17. "What contingency plans should I create for the highest-priority risks?"
18. "If this project were to fail, what would be the likely cause, and how can I prevent it now?"
19. "How can I involve the team in identifying potential risks they see from their perspectives?"
20. "What are the early warning signs that a risk is turning into an issue, and how can I monitor for them?"

Prompts for Innovation and Continuous Improvement

21. "What new tools or techniques can I introduce to make this project more efficient?"
22. "How can I foster a culture of creativity and experimentation within my project team?"
23. "What processes can I refine based on lessons learned from previous projects?"
24. "What small changes can I implement today to improve the team's workflow?"
25. "What trends or emerging technologies should I consider integrating into our project process?"

Prompts for Leadership and Team Management

26. "How can I support each team member to maximize their strengths on this project?"

27. "What steps can I take to build trust and rapport within the team?"
28. "How can I set realistic but challenging goals that inspire the team?"
29. "What behaviors should I model to foster a positive and productive work environment?"
30. "How can I recognize and celebrate the team's achievements, big or small?"

Prompts for Stakeholder Management

31. "What is the best way to align stakeholder expectations with project realities?"
32. "How can I keep stakeholders engaged without overwhelming them with details?"
33. "What key metrics or updates should I focus on in my next stakeholder report?"
34. "What strategies can I use to handle difficult or demanding stakeholders effectively?"
35. "How can I ensure all stakeholders feel their input is valued and considered?"

Prompts for Reflection and Growth

36. "What did I learn from the challenges faced in this project, and how can I improve moving forward?"
37. "How do I define success for this project beyond just meeting deliverables?"
38. "What are my strengths as a project manager, and how can I use them more effectively?"
39. "What feedback should I seek from my team to improve my leadership?"
40. "What legacy or long-term impact do I want this project to leave?"

These prompts are versatile and can be used for journaling, team discussions, AI brainstorming, or self-reflection to refine your project management approach. You can further tune based on the situations.

Appendix 2: Task Time Consumption Comparison

Here's a simple, practical template to capture and compare time consumption **with** and **without AI tools** for various tasks:

Project/Task Name: [Enter the name of the task or project]

Date: [Enter the date]

Task	Description	Time Spent Without AI (mins)	Time Spent With AI (mins)	Difference (mins)	Notes/ Observations
Task 1	[Brief description]	[e.g., 60]	[e.g., 15]	[e.g., 45]	[e.g., AI tool reduced repetitive work]
Task 2	[Brief description]	[e.g., 45]	[e.g., 20]	[e.g., 25]	[e.g., Faster data analysis]
Task 3	[Brief description]	[e.g., 30]	[e.g., 10]	[e.g., 20]	[e.g., Simplified formatting]

Total Time Saved: [Sum of all "Difference" values]

Key Insights:

1. [E.g., Overall percentage of time saved]
2. [E.g., Types of tasks where AI tools were most effective]
3. [E.g., Areas for further improvement or AI integration]

This format helps document the efficiency gained through AI tools while pinpointing areas where further optimization can occur.

"AI doesn't replace human intelligence; it amplifies it, enabling us to see what was once invisible."

— Ajay Tiwari

***

Chapter 1:

The AI Awakening: Demystifying the Tech

"The journey of a thousand miles begins with a single step, and understanding AI begins with a single spark of curiosity."

— Ajay Tiwari

The first rays of sunlight broke through the conference room window, painting streaks of gold on the table where Arjun sat. He was still processing the transformative potential of AI after his recent conversation with Krishna. The concept of an invisible ally guiding the chaos of developing a fully autonomous driving system had sparked both hope and skepticism in his mind.

Could such a system truly understand the nuances of vehicle dynamics, real-time sensor fusion, and predictive behavior modeling? Could it manage the avalanche of data streaming from LiDAR, cameras, and radar, while predicting and countering cyber threats aimed at autonomous vehicles? Or was it just another overhyped buzzword, exaggerated by sleek marketing campaigns?

The answers seemed tantalizingly close yet frustratingly distant.

As Arjun reached for his coffee, Krishna entered, holding a device resembling a miniature projector. With a grin, he set it on the table.

"Ready for the awakening?" Krishna asked, his voice brimming with anticipation.

"The awakening?" Arjun echoed, intrigued yet cautious.

"Yes," Krishna replied, pressing a button on the device. The room dimmed, and a holographic figure sprang to life, a sleek, humanoid representation of AI. Its form shimmered with streams of data, flowing like water through a crystalline matrix.

"This," Krishna said, gesturing to the figure, "is Maya, the embodiment of your invisible ally. She's here to help you demystify AI and reimagine the way you approach your project."

The holographic Maya turned to Arjun, her eyes glowing with an intelligent spark. "Hello, Arjun," she said, her voice smooth and reassuring. "I am here to guide you through the possibilities of artificial intelligence in your autonomous driving project."

Arjun leaned forward, curiosity mixed with skepticism. "You're telling me you can handle the complexities of a Level 5 autonomous driving system? Predict pedestrian behavior, avoid collisions, and counter cyber threats? All of it?"

Maya smiled, her demeanor confident but not condescending. "To understand my capabilities, you must first understand how I function. I am not just a machine; I am a system of systems. I learn, adapt, and evolve through algorithms, mathematical recipes - that grow smarter with experience. Let's start with my foundation: machine learning."

As Maya spoke, the hologram shifted, displaying vivid visualizations: busy city streets, interconnected sensor grids, and the complex architecture of autonomous systems.

"Machine learning," she began, "is the core of what I do. Imagine training a driver. At first, they rely on instructions and practice runs. Over time, with enough experience, they anticipate scenarios instinctively. Similarly, I learn from data patterns in vehicle behavior, road conditions, and pedestrian movements. The more I process, the more nuanced my decisions become."

Krishna interjected, "Do you remember the anomaly we encountered during the last safety simulation? Maya flagged it instantly, a misalignment in LiDAR data caused by environmental interference. That was supervised learning in action. She was trained on thousands of similar scenarios and recognized the pattern immediately."

"But how do you adapt to completely new situations?" Arjun asked.

Maya's hologram shifted to display a decision tree. "That's where reinforcement learning comes in. Think of it as trial and error, accelerated. I simulate countless scenarios and refine my strategies through feedback loops. For instance, in a chaotic urban environment, I test braking algorithms against simulated hazards until I determine the safest response."

The hologram shifted again, this time showing a neural network. "This," Maya continued, "is my brain. Neural networks enable me to interpret and analyze the complexities of real-time data, whether it's traffic flows or edge-case pedestrian behaviors."

Krishna leaned back, letting Arjun absorb the details. "You see," he said, "Maya doesn't replace your expertise—she amplifies it. By processing millions of data points in seconds, she identifies patterns and solutions that would take years for a human team to uncover."

Arjun folded his arms, his skepticism softening. "It sounds powerful, but isn't it risky? What happens when she's wrong?"

"Good question," Krishna replied. "AI isn't flawless, and that's why human oversight is essential. Think of Maya as a copilot, not a replacement. She complements your judgment with precision and scale."

Maya's tone grew serious. "There's another crucial element: data bias. My decisions are only as good as the data I am given. If that data is biased or incomplete, so are my conclusions."

Krishna elaborated, "For instance, if Maya were trained on datasets that didn't account for weather-related impacts on sensors, she might fail in heavy fog. That's why diverse and continually updated data are non-negotiable."

"So, you're saying I have to question your assumptions?" Arjun asked.

"Exactly," Maya replied. "We're partners, Arjun. Collaboration is the key to success."

Krishna loaded a test case into Maya. "Let me show you something real - a Level 5 prototype project I fed in."

The hologram transformed, displaying a detailed urban simulation. Maya began narrating: "In this scenario, the autonomous vehicle's decision engine failed to detect jaywalking pedestrians in low light. The system flagged environmental noise as the issue, but my analysis revealed the true problem - improper sensor calibration under dynamic lighting."

The simulation unfolded, showing Maya's diagnostics pinpointing the issue and recommending a recalibration protocol. "This optimization", Krishna said, "this will save weeks of trial-and-error and debugging."

Arjun's mind buzzed with possibilities. Could Maya bring the same clarity to his project? Could she mitigate risk, enhance safety, and accelerate development timelines?

"Let's test her," Arjun said, his skepticism now fueled by curiosity. "Load data from my autonomous driving platform. I want to see her in action."

Krishna smiled knowingly. "We will. But first, let's explore her predictive capabilities."

Maya presented a new scenario. "In autonomous systems," she explained, "predictive analytics can prevent accidents and optimize performance. By analyzing sensor data and historical traffic patterns, I forecast potential collisions and suggest proactive measures."

She demonstrated a prediction model where subtle deviations in GPS data hinted at a possible hardware failure. "Imagine," Maya said, "if I could warn you about this, weeks before it impacts operations."

Krishna added, "In a Level 5 system, split-second decisions can mean the difference between safety and catastrophe. Maya ensures those decisions are informed by data, not guesswork."

As the session concluded, Arjun felt a surge of excitement. Maya had transformed AI from a buzzword into a powerful ally. But questions remained, and he was eager to uncover the answers.

"Krishna," he said, "this is incredible, but where do I start? How do I make Maya an integral part of my team?"

Krishna smiled. "That's the next step. Remember, AI isn't here to replace you, it's here to empower you. Together, you and Maya will redefine what's possible in autonomous driving."

As Arjun left the room, his doubts had evolved into determination. The AI awakening had begun, and he was ready to embrace the journey ahead.

Summary

Arjun, a seasoned project manager, grapples with the daunting challenges of leading a Level 5 autonomous driving project. A conversation with Krishna, his innovative colleague, introduces him to the concept of AI as an "invisible ally" in project management.

The chapter unfolds with Krishna presenting Maya, a holographic representation of AI, who demystifies the technology by explaining its foundation in machine learning and neural networks. Through vivid examples, Arjun learns how Maya can process complex data, anticipate risks, and optimize solutions in ways that human teams cannot achieve alone.

Despite initial skepticism, Arjun's curiosity is piqued as he glimpses the transformative potential of AI to enhance decision-making, streamline workflows, and mitigate project risks. The chapter closes with Arjun eager to explore Maya's capabilities further, setting the stage for a deep dive into predictive analytics and AI-driven problem-solving.

ALLY

Ask Questions: Begin by identifying challenges in your projects and asking how AI can address them.

Learn the Basics: Understand AI's foundations and research its applications in your field.

Leverage Tools: Start small by using AI tools for automating repetitive tasks or analyzing data.

Yield Results: Implement AI in one area and measure its impact to build confidence in its potential.

Call to Action

As Arjun takes the first step in his AI journey, it's time to reflect on your own challenges. How could AI serve as your invisible ally?

- **Explore:** Research how AI is being applied in your field. Start small-find tools that automate repetitive tasks or uncover insights from data. Find the list of activities done by a PM, its corresponding tools, how it can be automated in Appendix 3.
- **Question:** What are the bottlenecks in your current projects? Can AI help you address them faster or more effectively? See the Appendix 4 for all the project management activities.
- **Act:** Identify one area in your work where AI could make an immediate impact. Take the first step toward integrating AI into your decision-making process.

Remember, the journey to harnessing AI begins with a single question: *What if you had an ally like Maya on your team?*

Appendix 3: Daily Activities of a Program/Project Manager and Automation Opportunities

Activity	Description	Automation Opportunities
Planning and Scheduling	- Define project goals, scope, and deliverables. - Create and update project schedules (e.g., Gantt charts, timelines). - Allocate resources and plan dependencies.	Use MS Project Copilot: a custom version of chatgpt for Scheduling and dependency mapping, Predictive analytics for timeline and resource estimates. You can start from scratch or upload your mpp https://chatgpt.com/g/g-QJEX24GmA-ms-project-copilot Further refine based on your knowledge.
Repetitive Tasks / Boring Tasks	- Documentation - Followups - Reporting to higher management on daily basis - Risks - Reviews	Documentation: Chatgpt Use prompts shared in the Appendix 1
Task Assignment and Monitoring	- Assign tasks to team members based on skills and workload.- Monitor task progress and adjust priorities as needed.	Task management platforms (e.g., Trello, Jira) streamline assignments and tracking. AI can suggest task distribution based on workload analysis.
Risk Management	- Identify potential risks in project scope, resources, and timelines. - Develop mitigation strategies.	AI tools analyze historical data to predict risks. Automated alerts for deviations in performance or critical milestones.
Communication	- Facilitate team meetings and status updates. - Report progress to stakeholders.	Chatbots or AI assistants generate automated progress reports. Collaboration tools (e.g., Slack, MS Teams) streamline communication and updates. AI can draft and summarize meeting notes.

Budget Management	- Track expenses against the budget. - Approve costs and ensure resource allocation aligns with financial constraints.	Tools like SAP, Oracle, or specialized budget tracking software provide real-time cost analysis and forecasting.
Documentation	- Maintain records of meetings, decisions, and deliverables. - Ensure compliance with project standards.	Automation tools like Confluence, azure wiki or Notion generate and organize documentation automatically.
Change Management	- Address changes in project scope or priorities. - Evaluate the impact of changes on resources and timelines.	AI-driven scenario analysis evaluates the impact of scope changes. Workflow automation tools (e.g., Zapier, Azure) manage change requests efficiently.
Performance Monitoring	- Track Key Performance Indicators (KPIs) such as on-time delivery, quality, and cost adherence. - Conduct team performance reviews.	Dashboards powered by AI (e.g., Power BI) provide real-time KPI tracking. Automated performance analysis with machine learning insights.
Stakeholder Management	- Engage stakeholders for approvals, feedback, and updates. - Build consensus and manage expectations.	CRM tools like Salesforce automate stakeholder engagement tracking. AI sentiment analysis helps gauge stakeholder feedback.
Team Development	- Conduct training sessions and address team morale. - Ensure alignment with project goals and individual growth.	LMS (Learning Management Systems) automate training programs. AI tools provide insights into team performance and suggest development opportunities.

This table highlights how automation can simplify and enhance project management efficiency, allowing managers to focus more on strategic decision-making and team leadership.

Appendix 4: Project Management Activities across knowledge areas & process groups

Process Group	Knowledge Area	Activity	Tools/Methods/Processes	Artifacts	Tools	Time Estimate
Initiating	Integration Management	Develop Project Charter	Templates, Stakeholder meetings, Expert judgment	Project Charter	Microsoft Word, Google Docs, Templates	1-2 days
	Stakeholder Management	Identify Stakeholders	Stakeholder analysis, Brainstor-ming, Interviews	Stakeholder Register, Stakeholder Analysis	Excel, Miro, Microsoft Teams	2-3 days
Planning	Scope Management	Define Scope	Work Breakdown Structure (WBS), Expert judgment	Project Scope State-ment, WBS	Microsoft Word, Excel, WBS Tools	3-5 days
	Schedule Management	Define Activities	Decompo-sition, Rolling Wave Planning, Milestone charts	Activity List, Milestone List	Microsoft Project, Smartsheet, Asana	2-3 days
	Schedule Management	Sequence Activities	Precedence Diagramming Method (PDM), Gantt chart	Project Schedule	Microsoft Project, Primavera P6, Excel	2-3 days
	Time Management	Estimate Activity Durations	Expert judgment, Parametric Estimating, Analogous Estimating	Duration Estimates	Microsoft Project, Excel, Smart-sheet	2-4 days

	Cost Management	Estimate Costs	Analogous Estimating, Bottom-Up Estimating, Parametric Estimating	Cost Estimates	Excel, Microsoft Project, Cost Estimating Tools	3-5 days
	Quality Management	Plan Quality Managment	Bench-marking, Cost-Benefit Analysis, Quality Audits	Quality Management Plan	Excel, Quality Control Tools, Minitab	2-3 days
	Resource Management	Plan Resource Management	Resource breakdown structure (RBS), Resource smoothing	Resource Management Plan	Resource Guru, Microsoft Project, Excel	2-4 days
	Communications Management	Plan Communications Management	Communication models, Communication matrix, Feedback loops	Communications Management Plan	Microsoft Teams, Slack, Google Workspace	2-3 days
	Risk Management	Plan Risk Management	Risk Breakdown Structure (RBS), Risk assessment techniques	Risk Management Plan, Risk Register	Risk Register Software, Excel, Monte Carlo Tools	3-5 days
	Procurement Management	Plan Procurement Management	Market research, Procurement strategy	Procurement Management Plan	SAP, Microsoft Project, Zoho Projects	3-4 days
Executing	Integration Management	Direct and Manage Project Work	Project management software, Meetings, Stakeholder engagement	Work Performance Reports, Change Requests	Microsoft Project, Asana, Basecamp	Ongoing (Through-out)
	Quality Management	Manage Quality	Quality control tools, Process analysis	Quality Metrics, Quality Control Reports	Minitab, Excel, Quality Management Tools	Ongoing (Through-out)

	Resource Management	Acquire Resources	Resource leveling, Virtual team collaboration	Resource Availability Report	Resource Guru, Microsoft Teams, Zoom	Ongoing (Through-out)
	Communications Management	Manage Communications	Status reports, Meetings, Project management software	Project Reports, Meeting Minutes	Slack, Microsoft Teams, Google Docs	Ongoing (Through-out)
	Risk Management	Implement Risk Responses	Risk mitigation planning, Contingency planning	Risk Response Plan, Updated Risk Register	Risk Register Software, Excel, Monte Carlo Tools	Ongoing (Through-out)
	Procurement Management	Conduct Procure ments	Bid analysis, Procurement documentation	Procurement Contracts, Vendor Evaluation	SAP Ariba, Microsoft Project, Excel	2-4 weeks
Monitoring & Controlling	Integration Management	Monitor and Control Project Work	Earned Value Management (EVM), Project performance reviews	Work Performance Reports, EVM Analysis	Microsoft Project, Smartsheet, Power BI	Ongoing (Through-out)
	Scope Management	Validate Scope	Inspection, Control charts, Scope verification	Accepted Deliverables	Excel, Quality Control Tools, Miro	Ongoing (Through-out)
	Schedule Management	Control Schedule	Gantt charts, Project management software, Critical Path Method	Schedule Variance Report	Microsoft Project, Primavera P6, Smart-sheet	Ongoing (Through-out)
	Cost Management	Control Costs	EVM, Forecasting, Trend analysis	Cost Performance Report	Microsoft Project, Excel, Power BI	Ongoing (Through-out)

	Quality Management	Control Quality	Control charts, Statistical sampling, Inspections	Quality Reports	Minitab, Excel, Quality Control Tools	Ongoing (Through-out)
	Resource Management	Control Resources	Resource leveling, Resource histogram, Resource smoothing	Resource Utilization Report	Microsoft Project, Excel, Resource Guru	Ongoing (Through-out)
	Communications Management	Monitor Communications	Surveys, Feedback loops, Communi-cation audits	Communication Logs, Stakeholder Feedback	Microsoft Teams, Slack, Google Forms	Ongoing (Through-out)
	Risk Management	Monitor Risks	Risk audits, Risk reviews, Status meetings	Risk Register, Risk Response Plan Updates	Risk Register Software, Excel, Monte Carlo Tools	Ongoing (Through-out)
	Procurement Management	Control Procurements	Contract monitoring, Performance reviews, Inspections	Procurement Performance Reports	SAP, Microsoft Project, Zoho Projects	Ongoing (Through-out)
Closing	Integration Management	Close Project or Phase	Lessons learned, Final project review, Final deliverables review	Final Product Deliverables, Lessons Learned	Microsoft Word, Excel, Conflu-ence	1-2 weeks
	Procurement Management	Close Procurements	Procurement audits, Contract closure	Procurement Closure Documents	SAP, Microsoft Project, Zoho Projects	1 week

Chapter 2

The Silent Project Killer

"Technology is not just about machines; it's about unleashing human potential to do what was once impossible."

— Krishna Mehra

"Tools are only as powerful as the hands that wield them."

— Ajay Tiwari

After few months into the project, one morning Arjun was staring at the project schedule and was thinking why its delaying even after meticulous planning and support from Maya. Arjun felt the weight of his responsibilities even more pressing. As he sat down with his laptop further, the project's timeline in front of him, Arjun's mind was consumed by an all-too-familiar problem: scope creep.

It had already begun to rear its ugly head in his autonomous driving project, a challenge that had the potential to derail months of hard work. There were constant requests from stakeholders for additional features, functionalities, and integration with new technologies. What started as a Level 5 autonomous driving system had slowly morphed into something far more complex than originally planned. He pinged Krishna for assistance.

Meanwhile Arjun muttered to himself, "How do I keep this in check?"

In a short while, his phone buzzed. It was a message from Krishna: "Ready for the next step? Let's talk about tools to tackle your real challenges."

Arjun's heart raced. Was it possible that AI could truly help him with scope creep? He was about to find out.

As Arjun joined the video call, Krishna's familiar face appeared on the screen, but this time, Maya wasn't far behind. The hologram of Maya flickered to life beside Krishna, her form shimmering as always, exuding a calm assurance.

"Good morning, Arjun. I hear you're facing some challenges," Maya said, her voice filled with empathy.

"You could say that," Arjun replied with a sigh. "Scope creep is eating away at our timeline, and I don't know how to manage all the shifting requirements while staying within budget."

Maya nodded, her eyes sparkling with understanding. "Scope creep is one of the most common pain points for project managers.

It often sneaks in under the guise of new opportunities, but without careful management, it can completely disrupt a project."

Krishna leaned forward. "You've probably tried using traditional methods like change requests or scope documentation, but those can be time-consuming and ineffective if the changes keep coming in fast."

Arjun nodded. "Exactly. Every time we add a new feature or requirement, the schedule gets pushed back, and the budget gets strained."

Maya's hologram shifted, and a detailed flowchart appeared in the air.

"That's where I come in," she said. "With AI-powered tools, we can not only track scope creep but also predict it before it derails your project."

Arjun watched, intrigued, as Maya explained the first tool in her arsenal: predictive analytics.

"Predictive analytics can give you insights into how likely scope creep is to occur, based on historical data and trends. For instance, by analyzing past projects and their scope changes, I can identify early warning signs in your current project," Maya explained.

She pulled up a graph on the screen. "Here, we can see the frequency of scope changes in your project compared to similar projects in your industry. You're currently trending above the average, which means there's a higher likelihood that additional changes will continue to impact your timeline."

Arjun's eyebrows furrowed. "So, you're telling me you can predict scope creep before it even happens?"

"Yes," Maya replied, her tone confident. "Using historical data, I can spot patterns in stakeholder requests, feature additions, and project changes. Once I understand these patterns, I can forecast which areas of the project are most vulnerable to scope creep, and we can take preemptive action to avoid delays."

Arjun leaned back, trying to process the implications. Could this be the solution he had been searching for? Could AI truly provide him with the foresight to manage scope creep effectively?

Krishna jumped in. "And it doesn't stop there. Predictive tools like these can also integrate with your scheduling and budgeting systems, so you can adjust timelines and costs before a problem fully materializes."

Maya's hologram shifted once more, and a new interface appeared. "This tool connects to your project management platform. As it receives real-time data from your project activities, it continuously analyzes potential risk factors."

Arjun looked at the screen, seeing how Maya was able to identify a potential bottleneck based on resource allocation. "For example," Maya continued, "let's say there's a sudden surge in requests for additional features from a stakeholder. My system would flag this as a potential source of scope creep and suggest a more manageable course of action - whether that's delaying certain features or reallocating resources."

Krishna added, "By using AI to track project activities and analyze patterns, we can proactively adjust project plans, update schedules, and reallocate resources in response to emerging risks. This allows you to keep your project on track without compromising quality or burning through your budget."

Arjun could already see how this approach would allow him to stay ahead of the curve. He wouldn't have to wait until scope creep had already derailed the project - AI would give him the insight he needed to act before things got out of hand.

The conversation turned to the next crucial step in Arjun's journey—making his first AI-driven "tech choice." Krishna explained that the next phase of AI implementation was about selecting the right tool for the right challenge.

"AI tools come in many shapes and sizes," Krishna said. "Some focus on scheduling and resource management, others on risk prediction or stakeholder analysis. The key is identifying the problem you're facing and choosing the tool that best fits your needs."

Maya added, "Let's break it down. If you're struggling with scope creep, predictive analytics might be your first tool. If budget overruns are the main challenge, AI-driven budgeting tools that track expenses and suggest adjustments might be more appropriate."

Arjun thought about his current project. Scope creep was certainly a challenge, but there was also the issue of managing the vast amounts of data his team was handling on a daily basis. He would need to explore tools that could both predict risks and optimize resource usage.

Krishna smiled, sensing Arjun's thought process. "Exactly. Now, it's time to make that first tech choice. What will be your tool to handle scope creep?"

Arjun felt the weight of that decision. But with Maya's guidance, he felt confident that this first step would help him move closer to his goal.

The discussion wrapped up with Maya offering one final piece of advice. "Remember, the power of AI is not in one tool alone. It's about integrating multiple tools to create a comprehensive system that tackles different aspects of your project. Start with one tool, but always keep an eye on others that could help along the way."

Arjun nodded, feeling both energized and overwhelmed. The road ahead was long, but with the right tools and AI as his ally, he knew he had the potential to manage his project with a precision he never thought possible.

As he signed off, Arjun felt a renewed sense of purpose. The AI journey had truly begun, and he was ready to face the challenges of his autonomous driving project with newfound confidence and clarity.

Summary

Arjun grapples with scope creep in his Level 5 autonomous driving project and discovers how AI can help predict and manage it. Through predictive analytics, AI tools can identify early signs of scope creep by analyzing historical data and trends, allowing project managers to take preemptive action. Maya introduces the concept of selecting the right AI tools for specific project challenges, empowering Arjun to make an informed decision on how to tackle his project's pain points. As Arjun explores the possibilities, he gains confidence in using AI to manage risk, optimize resources, and keep his project on track.

S.P.A.R.K.

As Arjun has taken the first step in utilizing AI to manage scope creep, it's time for you to consider your own project.

- **S**earch: What's the biggest challenge you're facing in your project today? Is it scope creep, budget issues, or risk management?
- **P**redict: Leverage AI tools to analyze historical data and trends in your projects, just like Arjun.
- **A**ct: Choose one AI tool that addresses your current pain point and start integrating it into your project management processes.
- **R**eflect: Regularly assess how your AI tools are improving your project management practices.
- **K**eep Evolving: As your project progresses, look for new AI tools that can help you manage other aspects of your work.

Remember, the first step in embracing AI is deciding where to start. Once you've chosen your first tool, the journey ahead will unfold with more clarity and precision. Let AI guide you to success!

See the Appendix 5 on how to handle scope creep effectively and Appendix 6 on how to handle scope creep with limited input from customers.

Appendix 5: Managing Scope Creep Holistically with Examples

Scope creep occurs when unplanned changes expand the scope of a project, leading to delays, cost overruns, or quality compromises. Here's a table to help understand what contributes to scope creep, what goes unnoticed, the problems it causes, and actionable solutions. Managing scope creep with customers requires a balance of diplomacy, transparency, and firm adherence to agreed-upon processes. Below is a framework, supplemented with examples, for managing scope creep in customer interactions effectively and post that how to handle it holistically has been shared,

Contributors to Scope Creep	Examples	Problems Faced	Solutions	Actionable Steps
Unclear Initial Scope	- Ambiguous project requirements-Incomplete or vague SOW (Statement of Work) - Customer requests additional features claiming they were "implied" in initial discussions.	- Misaligned expectations. - Frequent rework and revisions. - Ensure detailed documentation of requirements.-Conduct a scope review before project commencement. - Gain written agreement from the customer.	- Use a detailed scope statement with clear deliverables. - Define what is excluded explicitly - In our initial agreement, we outlined X, Y, and Z as deliverables. If A and B are required, we can assess their impact on the project timeline."	- Workshop with stakeholders to align on requirements. - Use AI tools to identify gaps in scope definition.
Frequent Change Requests	- Customer frequently adds small changes, disrupting timelines and focus.	- Implement a formal change request process. - Set expectations for timeline and cost impacts of changes.	"We can certainly add this feature. Let's assess how it impacts the schedule and cost, and I'll send over an updated proposal."	- Create a change request log. - Provide an impact analysis

Stakeholder Changes	-Stakeholders request additional features after project initiation.	- New requests impact project timelines and budgets. - Difficulty in managing priorities.	- Establish a formal change request process. - Use decision frameworks (e.g., MoSCoW or Eisenhower Matrix) to evaluate change requests.	- Create a change request log. - Provide cost/impact analysis for each new request.
Overenthu-siastic Team	- Team adds extra features to "improve" the product. - Implementing suggestions without approval.	- Delays in the original timeline. - Increased costs due to unapproved changes.	- Foster a culture of discipline. - Reinforce the importance of adhering to the approved scope.	- Use retrospectives to identify and discuss unapproved changes. - Track work against deliverables using project management tools.
Inadequate Change Control	- Lack of a process for documenting and approving scope changes.	- Chaos in managing multiple changes. - Resources stretched thin without planning.	- Implement a robust change control process. - Maintain a log of all change requests with their impacts documented.	- Train the team on change control processes. - Use templates for change request documentation.
External Factors	- Regulatory updates during the project. - Market changes demanding quick pivots.	- Last-minute changes derail schedules. - Budget revisions cause conflict with stakeholders.	- Build contingency plans. - Allocate buffer time and budget for unforeseen changes.	- Schedule periodic reviews to assess external factors. - Use AI predictive tools to foresee potential market or regulatory impacts.

Customer Assumes Free Additions	- Customer assumes minor changes can be added without affecting cost or time.	- Explain the impact of even small changes. - Use data to showcase the trade-offs involved.	"Even minor changes require re-testing the whole module, which adds 3 extra days. Let's discuss if we want to prioritize this."	1. Define and Communicate the SOW: Draft a detailed Statement of Work outlining deliverables, exclusions, and acceptance criteria, then secure formal sign-off before starting work. 2. Enforce Change Requests: Require all new feature requests to go through a documented change control process, including impact analysis on time and cost. 3. Set Cost Thresholds: Establish budget ceilings for additional work and communicate the costs for any out-of-scope items
Unplanned Stakeholder Involvement	- New stakeholders from the customer's side suggest changes late in the project.	- Involve all stakeholders during the planning phase. - Set clear rules for late-stage requests and how they will be handled.	"We value your input. However, as we're in the implementation phase, any changes now would require us to revisit the schedule and budget."	1. Stakeholder Register Early: Identify all potential stakeholders at project kickoff, mapping their roles and decision-making authority. 2. RACI Matrix: Define who is Responsible, Accountable, Consulted, and Informed for each deliverable to prevent informal approvals. 3. Formalize Late Requests: Treat new stakeholder inputs as change requests, requiring the same approval and impact evaluation.

Scope Expands Without Budget	- Customer requests more features but resists increasing the budget.	- Communicate transparently about cost implications. - Provide a breakdown of resources and costs for new features.	"To accommodate these new features, we'd need an additional $10,000. Let's discuss how we can adjust the current scope to fit the budget."	1. Link Scope to Budget: For every deliverable, specify associated costs and require budget approval for changes. 2. Threshold Alerts: Configure automated alerts when spending approaches defined thresholds, prompting review. 3. Cost-Benefit Evaluation: For any new feature, present a cost-benefit analysis to stakeholders before approval.
Undefined Dependencies	- Customer requests features without understan-ding dependencies with other systems or teams.	- Use dependency mapping to explain the effort required. - Schedule walkthroughs to align on technical complexities.	"This feature requires integration with X. Adding it would involve coordination with Y team, which adds complexity. Let's evaluate together."	1. Dependency Mapping: Create a Work Breakdown Structure (WBS) that explicitly lists task dependencies and hand-offs. 2. Use Scheduling Tools: Leverage project software to visualize and lock dependencies, triggering alerts for any unsanctioned changes. 3. Periodic Reviews: Regularly review dependency logs to catch new or shifted relationships before they cause delay.

During the scope creep what gets unnoticed are listed below with their actionable steps,

What Gets Unnoticed?	Examples	Problems Faced	Solutions	Actionable Steps
Hidden Resource Strain	- Small additions to tasks for each team member. - Overlapping responsibilities not accounted for.	- Reduced efficiency. - Delays in completing tasks.	- Use resource management tools to track workloads. - Redistribute tasks when resource strain is identified.	- Review team workload weekly. - Implement a workload balancing system.
Uncaptured Downstream Impact	- A change in one module affecting other interconnected systems or deliverables.	- Delays and budget overruns in dependent areas. - Unplanned rework across multiple teams.	- Use dependency tracking tools. - Conduct impact analysis for each change request.	- Map depende-ncies in the project plan.- Create a checklist for assessing change impacts.
Silent Approvals	- Team members make changes without consulting managers. - Changes are communicated informally and not documented.	- Project deviates from the original plan.- Reduced control over scope and outcomes.	- Establish clear approval hierarchies. - Encourage open communication about changes.	- Create and enforce a formal approval process. - Use a shared platform to track and document changes.
Team Morale and Fatigue	- Team works overtime to accommodate new changes.- Lack of clarity causes stress and burnout.	- Decreased productivity.- Increased turnover or disengage-ment.	- Monitor team well-being through regular check-ins. - Adjust timelines or reassign tasks as needed.	- Schedule breaks and celebrate milestones. - Conduct anonymous feedback surveys to gauge team morale.

Step-by-Step Process to solve the scope creep

What Gets Unnoticed?	Examples	Problems Faced	Solutions	Actionable Steps
Hidden Resource Strain	- Small additions to tasks for each team member. - Overlapping responsibi-lities not accounted for.	- Reduced efficiency. - Delays in completing tasks.	- Use resource management tools to track workloads. - Redistribute tasks when resource strain is identified.	- Review team workload weekly. - Implement a workload balancing system.
Uncaptured Downstream Impact	- A change in one module affecting other interconnected systems or deliverables.	- Delays and budget overruns in dependent areas. - Unplanned rework across multiple teams.	- Use dependency tracking tools. - Conduct impact analysis for each change request.	- Map dependencies in the project plan. - Create a checklist for assessing change impacts.
Silent Approvals	- Team members make changes without consulting managers. - Changes are communicated informally and not documented.	- Project deviates from the original plan. - Reduced control over scope and outcomes.	- Establish clear approval hierarchies. - Encourage open communication about changes.	- Create and enforce a formal approval process. - Use a shared platform to track and document changes.
Team Morale and Fatigue	- Team works overtime to accommodate new changes. - Lack of clarity causes stress and burnout.	- Decreased productivity. - Increased turnover or disengage-ment.	- Monitor team well-being through regular check-ins. - Adjust timelines or reassign tasks as needed.	- Schedule breaks and celebrate milestones. - Conduct anonymous feedback surveys to gauge team morale.

Step-by-Step Guide for effective Customer Engagement

Step	Actions	Example Communication
Step 1: Set Clear Expectations	- During project initiation, define deliverables and exclusions explicitly.- Document all agreements in contracts and SOW.	"We'll deliver X, Y, and Z as outlined, with timelines as discussed. Any changes to this scope will follow the formal process outlined."
Step 2: Educate the Customer	- Explain the impact of scope creep in terms of time, cost, and quality. - Use visual aids like timelines or budget graphs.	"Adding this feature will push the timeline by 2 weeks and increase costs by $5,000. Would you like me to draft a proposal for approval?"
Step 3: Formalize the Change Process	- Create a structured process for change requests, including documentation, approval, and updated timelines.	"Here's the form for submitting change requests. Once approved, we'll incorporate the changes into the project schedule and cost."
Step 4: Negotiate Trade-offs	- Encourage the customer to prioritize changes by swapping out lower-priority items or extending timelines.	"If we add Feature A, we may need to delay Feature B or increase the timeline. Which would you prefer?"
Step 5: Provide Regular Updates	- Use project status reports to keep customers informed about progress, challenges, and potential impacts of requested changes.	"As of today, we are on track. However, integrating the requested feature will require re-testing, potentially delaying delivery."
Step 6: Maintain Flexibility with Boundaries	- Be accommodating but firm about adhering to processes. - Always link changes to their impact on the overall project.	"We understand this is important. However, without adjusting the timeline or resources, quality might be compromised."
Step 7: Post-Project Reflection	- Conduct a review with the customer to discuss lessons learned and improve future collaboration.	"Looking back, aligning early on scope details reduced delays. For future projects, we could enhance this by X."

Using AI to Support Customer Interactions

Step	Actions	Example Communication
Step 1: Set Clear Expectations	- During project initiation, define deliverables and exclusions explicitly.- Document all agreements in contracts and SOW.	"We'll deliver X, Y, and Z as outlined, with timelines as discussed. Any changes to this scope will follow the formal process outlined."
Step 2: Educate the Customer	- Explain the impact of scope creep in terms of time, cost, and quality. - Use visual aids like timelines or budget graphs.	"Adding this feature will push the timeline by 2 weeks and increase costs by $5,000. Would you like me to draft a proposal for approval?"
Step 3: Formalize the Change Process	- Create a structured process for change requests, including documentation, approval, and updated timelines.	"Here's the form for submitting change requests. Once approved, we'll incorporate the changes into the project schedule and cost."
Step 4: Negotiate Trade-offs	- Encourage the customer to prioritize changes by swapping out lower-priority items or extending timelines.	"If we add Feature A, we may need to delay Feature B or increase the timeline. Which would you prefer?"
Step 5: Provide Regular Updates	- Use project status reports to keep customers informed about progress, challenges, and potential impacts of requested changes.	"As of today, we are on track. However, integrating the requested feature will require re-testing, potentially delaying delivery."
Step 6: Maintain Flexibility with Boundaries	- Be accommodating but firm about adhering to processes. - Always link changes to their impact on the overall project.	"We understand this is important. However, without adjusting the timeline or resources, quality might be compromised."
Step 7: Post-Project Reflection	- Conduct a review with the customer to discuss lessons learned and improve future collaboration.	"Looking back, aligning early on scope details reduced delays. For future projects, we could enhance this by X."

Key Communication Principles for Managing Scope Creep with Customers

1. **Transparency:** Always explain the impact of requested changes in terms of cost, time, and quality. Use data and visuals to support your argument.
2. **Empathy:** Understand the customer's underlying needs behind change requests and address those directly.
3. **Proactivity:** Anticipate potential misunderstandings and address them before they escalate.
4. **Consistency:** Follow the agreed-upon change control process without exceptions, reinforcing its importance to stakeholders.
5. **Firmness with Diplomacy:** Be firm about boundaries but offer alternatives to demonstrate flexibility and willingness to collaborate.

By combining structured processes, AI tools, and clear communication, you can manage scope creep effectively while maintaining a positive customer relationship.

This holistic approach, when paired with practical tools and AI insights, enables project managers to identify, address, and mitigate scope creep while maintaining project integrity and team morale.

Appendix 6: Defining Scope Clearly with Limited Customer Input

When customers provide only top-level information, defining a detailed project scope becomes challenging but not impossible. A systematic approach can clarify expectations, establish boundaries, and prevent scope creep. Here's how:

Steps to Define Scope Clearly

Step	Actions	Example
1. Conduct Discovery Sessions	- Organize workshops or interviews to gather more details. - Use brainstorming and mind-mapping to uncover customer expectations.	"Let's break down the high-level goal of 'enhanced user experience' into specific deliverables, like improved navigation, faster load times, and a personalized dashboard."
2. Use Visual Tools	- Create mockups, prototypes, or process flow diagrams to visualize potential deliverables. - Use these to elicit more detailed feedback.	"Here's a wireframe of the dashboard based on your description. Can you confirm if this aligns with your vision or highlight what's missing?"
3. Establish Assumptions	- Document all assumptions underlying the scope to make gaps explicit. - Clarify with the customer that these assumptions are open to revision.	"We're assuming the project involves developing a mobile app, integrating payment systems, and ensuring compatibility with both Android and iOS. Are these assumptions correct?"
4. Define Objectives and Exclusions	- Clearly outline what the project will achieve (objectives) and what it will not cover (exclusions).	"This project will include a product catalog and search functionality. However, live inventory tracking and customer reviews are excluded unless explicitly added in a change request."
5. Create a Detailed SOW (Statement of Work)	- Draft an SOW that includes deliverables, timelines, milestones, and acceptance criteria. - Highlight dependencies and risks.	"The deliverables include a web platform with user authentication and a content management system by June 30th. The customer must provide all content by May 15th to meet this deadline."

6. Establish Change Control	- Define a formal process for handling changes to scope. - Include impact analysis for time, cost, and resources.	"Any additions to the scope will require a change request form, followed by a review of how it impacts the timeline and budget. Only approved changes will be incorporated into the project."
7. Use Progressive Elaboration	- Start with broad deliverables and refine them as the project progresses, using customer feedback to adjust details.	"Initially, we'll focus on building the core functionalities. As we gather feedback, we'll define additional features like custom reporting or advanced analytics."

Setting Boundaries and Communicating Them

Boundary Type	How to Set It	Example Communication
Deliverables	- Clearly list what will be delivered and in what format.	"We'll deliver a fully functioning e-commerce website with product listing, payment integration, and order tracking."
Timeframes	- Provide a detailed timeline with milestones.- Highlight dependencies on customer inputs.	"The project timeline is contingent on receiving final product specifications by March 15th. Delays will impact delivery."
Budget	- Specify costs for the defined scope and outline a separate pricing structure for additional work.	"This budget covers only the outlined features. Any additional features will be billed at an agreed hourly rate of $100."
Quality Standards	- Define measurable quality criteria for deliverables.	"The deliverables will meet performance benchmarks such as page load speed under 3 seconds and 99.9% uptime."
Roles and Responsibilities	- Outline the responsibilities of both parties to prevent ambiguity.	"Our team will handle development, while your team will provide branding guidelines and approve wireframes within 3 days."

How AI Can Help Define Scope

Boundary Type	How to Set It	Example Communication
Deliverables	- Clearly list what will be delivered and in what format.	"We'll deliver a fully functioning e-commerce website with product listing, payment integration, and order tracking."
Timeframes	- Provide a detailed timeline with milestones. - Highlight dependencies on customer inputs.	"The project timeline is contingent on receiving final product specifications by March 15th. Delays will impact delivery."
Budget	- Specify costs for the defined scope and outline a separate pricing structure for additional work.	"This budget covers only the outlined features. Any additional features will be billed at an agreed hourly rate of $100."
Quality Standards	- Define measurable quality criteria for deliverables.	"The deliverables will meet performance benchmarks such as page load speed under 3 seconds and 99.9% uptime."
Roles and Responsibilities	- Outline the responsibilities of both parties to prevent ambiguity.	"Our team will handle development, while your team will provide branding guidelines and approve wireframes within 3 days."

By following these steps and principles, you can effectively define the scope even with minimal initial input, establish clear boundaries, and ensure smooth customer collaboration throughout the project lifecycle.

"The right tool, when used correctly, can turn a daunting project into a series of manageable tasks."

— Ajay Tiwari

***

Chapter 3

The Oracle of Planning

"The future belongs to those who can see it coming and act before it arrives."

— Ajay Tiwari

"In the world of uncertainty, the best plans are not those that predict the future, but those that adapt to it."

— Ajay Tiwari

The soft hum of the AI workstation filled the room as Arjun sat back in his chair, staring at the wall of monitors before him. The office lights flickered gently above, but his mind was elsewhere focused on the project that had consumed him for months. The Level 5 autonomous vehicle prototype had reached its critical phase, and every decision seemed more crucial than the last. He had often felt like a juggler in the midst of a storm, keeping an eye on the schedule, resources, quality, and risk, but always wondering if there was a better way to foresee the obstacles ahead.

As he rubbed his temple, Krishna entered the room with a broad smile on his face. “You look like you’ve had a long day,” he said, taking a seat beside Arjun.

“You could say that,” Arjun replied with a half-smile. “The complexities of this autonomous driving project are making my head spin. I’m just not sure if our plan is solid enough to carry us through the next phase.”

Krishna leaned back, tapping his fingers on the table thoughtfully. “Have you checked with Maya for help”.

Arjun’s curiosity piqued. “Maya? What’s she got to do with planning?”

“You’re thinking too small, Arjun. Think of Maya not just as an assistant, but as the Oracle of Planning. You know, like those ancient oracles that would predict the future, offering wisdom that shaped the course of decisions? Maya does the same thing, only she uses data instead of prophecies.”

Arjun raised an eyebrow. “So, she predicts the future of our project?”

Krishna smiled. “Not quite that simple. But she certainly offers insights that can help you see the future of your project more clearly, with far more accuracy than we’ve been able to before.”

Maya materialized before them, her holographic form shimmering with the elegance of flowing data. She projected a warm, welcoming presence, but there was something distinctly powerful about the way she stood. The environment in the room subtly shifted, as though her presence had turned the space into something more… futuristic.

“Hello, Arjun,” Maya said, her voice carrying the calm assurance of someone who had seen countless projects come to fruition.

“Ready to get started?” Krishna asked, leaning forward, eager to see Arjun’s reaction.

Arjun nodded, unsure of what he expected, but intrigued nonetheless. “Alright, Oracle. What’s your plan?”

Maya’s holographic form flickered and expanded, revealing a detailed project timeline, complete with resource allocations and potential risks.

“Let’s start with the basics. I can analyze historical data—data from past projects, market conditions, team performance, and external factors like weather patterns or industry trends and use it to forecast potential paths your project might take.”

Arjun watched, spellbound, as Maya’s interface began to pull in massive amounts of data, all of it flowing together in a seamless dance of lights and numbers.

“Now,” Maya continued, “let’s look at your timeline. Based on historical patterns, I can forecast delays due to various factors, whether it’s resource shortages, unexpected technical hurdles, or even market shifts that could impact your budget or schedules. I’ll also suggest the optimal allocation of your resources based on team expertise, previous project performance, and the complexity of each task.”

Krishna leaned in. “It’s like consulting an oracle that knows not just what *could* happen, but also what *should* happen, based on everything we’ve learned so far.”

Arjun rubbed his chin. “But how do I know the predictions are accurate? We’ve had AI systems give us predictions before, and they’ve been wrong more times than I care to remember.”

Maya smiled. “Good question. The key to my accuracy is continuous learning. Every time a new variable enters the system, I analyze it and update my forecast. Just like with machine learning, the more data I have, the smarter I become. Think of me as your continuous guide, constantly recalibrating as new information flows in."

The AI interface shifted once again, showing a real-time simulation of Arjun's autonomous driving project, superimposed with potential future outcomes. It was as though he were looking into a crystal ball, but instead of ethereal wisps of smoke, the vision was grounded in hard data.

"Here's a prediction," Maya said, her voice steady. "You're entering a critical phase of the project where the integration of hardware and software will be a huge bottleneck. Based on past projects, this is a typical place where most teams experience delays either because of unforeseen technical complications or resource limitations. My prediction? You'll need an additional software developer for the next sprint if you want to meet your timeline. I suggest reallocating one of your engineers from testing to assist with this."

Arjun blinked. It was spot on. He hadn't even considered the bottleneck that Maya had just identified. "And if I don't do it?" Arjun asked, his voice tinged with curiosity.

"If you don't," Maya replied, "there's a 65% chance your project will experience a delay of at least three weeks. The risk? A delay in software development could cause a domino effect pushing back testing schedules and ultimately delaying the overall delivery."

Arjun's eyes widened. "This is... uncanny."

Krishna grinned. "That's the magic of AI-powered planning. It's not just about predicting the future. It's about giving you the tools to shape it proactively.

Arjun began to feel the weight of Maya's insights. This wasn't just about receiving a forecast. It was about using that forecast to make smarter, more informed decisions.

Maya continued, "A robust plan isn't just a static document, it's a dynamic one, shaped by real-time inputs. I'll show you how to adjust your resources based on evolving circumstances. For example, if a key vendor falls behind schedule, I'll suggest a buffer period where tasks can be rescheduled or redistributed to prevent further delays."

Arjun watched as Maya quickly adjusted the timeline, shifting resources and optimizing the schedule in real-time, ensuring that all aspects of the project remained balanced.

"And here's another advantage," Maya said. "I can predict the likelihood of certain risks materializing - such as delays due to external market conditions. If there's a sudden shift in global supply chains or new regulations affecting autonomous vehicles, I'll flag it early. You'll have time to adjust, to prepare. Think of me as your early warning system, giving you the time and space to react before problems escalate."

Arjun took it all in. "So you're saying, with you on the team, I can build plans that are not only reactive but also proactive?"

"Exactly," Maya replied. "I'm not here just to predict the future. I'm here to help you shape it, to build a more adaptable and resilient plan that can withstand whatever challenges may come your way."

Arjun now understood the depth of what Maya could offer. This wasn't some futuristic dream; this was the reality of AI-powered planning. But how could he take this knowledge and apply it directly to his project?

"Alright," Arjun said, standing up. "Let's make this actionable. What's the first step?"

Krishna leaned forward, offering practical advice. "Start by feeding as much historical data as possible into the system. The more information Maya has, the more accurate the forecasts will be. Look for patterns, patterns in resource allocation, in timelines, in risks and use those insights to build a more adaptable plan."

Arjun nodded, feeling a surge of confidence. "Got it. I can see how this could change everything. But what about the human side of things? How do I balance this powerful AI tool with the team's judgment and expertise?"

Maya's voice softened. "The human touch is still essential. I am here to guide you, but the final decisions should always involve human intuition and expertise. The key is collaboration working alongside me, rather than relying on me alone."

As Arjun looked at the updated plan on the screen, he couldn't help but feel a sense of relief. For the first time in months, he could see a clear path forward. The predictions were not just data they were a roadmap for success.

"Thank you, Maya," Arjun said, his voice filled with newfound respect. "You've given me a new perspective on planning. I'm excited to see how this plays out."

Krishna smiled. "Remember, Arjun, the future is always in motion. It's not about predicting every detail. It's about staying flexible and responsive to the changes that come your way. With AI on your side, you'll always be one step ahead."

Summary

In this chapter, Arjun learns how AI, embodied by Maya, acts as an "Oracle of Planning," providing powerful predictive insights that shape the course of the autonomous driving project. Maya uses historical data to forecast potential risks, resource needs, and project timelines, offering solutions to make Arjun's plans more adaptable and robust. By continuously learning and updating predictions, Maya empowers Arjun to build smarter, proactive plans and identify risks before they become critical.

Key Takeaways:

- AI's predictive capabilities provide a clearer, data-driven roadmap for projects.
- Use historical data to build more adaptable and resilient plans.
- Collaboration with AI strengthens decision-making, but human intuition remains essential.

P.A.C.E.

- **P**redict: Utilize AI to forecast potential outcomes and risks.
- **A**dapt: Build flexible plans that can adjust to new information and changing conditions.
- **C**ollaborate: Combine AI insights with human judgment for optimal decision-making.
- **E**valuate: Continuously evaluate and update plans based on real-time data to stay ahead.

By integrating these strategies into your planning approach, you can unlock the power of AI to lead your projects with precision and foresight, much like consulting an oracle who can guide you toward success. As you reflect on your own projects, you can start incorporating AI-powered planning into your strategy. Begin by gathering historical data from previous projects or similar ones to feed into your planning systems. Use this information to forecast potential risks, bottlenecks, and opportunities, ensuring that your plans are flexible and adaptive to changing conditions. Consider adopting an AI assistant like Maya, who not only predicts future scenarios but continuously updates forecasts based on real-time information. This will allow you to make proactive decisions, optimize resource allocation, and ultimately deliver projects more efficiently.

Use the Appendix 7 on how to effectively do project planning.

Appendix 7: Effective Project Planning with AI: A Step-by-Step Guide

AI can revolutionize project planning by providing data-driven insights, automating repetitive tasks, and improving decision-making. Here's how you can effectively leverage AI to plan a project:

Boundary Type	How to Set It	Example Communication
Deliverables	- Clearly list what will be delivered and in what format.	"We'll deliver a fully functioning e-commerce website with product listing, payment integration, and order tracking."
Timeframes	- Provide a detailed timeline with milestones. - Highlight dependencies on customer inputs.	"The project timeline is contingent on receiving final product specifications by March 15th. Delays will impact delivery."
Budget	- Specify costs for the defined scope and outline a separate pricing structure for additional work.	"This budget covers only the outlined features. Any additional features will be billed at an agreed hourly rate of $100."
Quality Standards	- Define measurable quality criteria for deliverables.	"The deliverables will meet performance benchmarks such as page load speed under 3 seconds and 99.9% uptime."
Roles and Responsibilities	- Outline the responsibilities of both parties to prevent ambiguity.	"Our team will handle development, while your team will provide branding guidelines and approve wireframes within 3 days."

AI Capabilities to Enhance Project Planning

Capability	How It Helps	Example Use Case
Natural Language Processing	Understands and interprets project documentation, creating summaries or detailed plans.	"ChatGPT analyzes the project charter and generates an initial project plan."
Predictive Analytics	Analyzes trends and historical data to forecast risks and timelines.	"AI predicts a 20% likelihood of delay due to resource unavailability."
Scenario Analysis	Simulates multiple scenarios to optimize planning decisions.	"If Task A is delayed, AI suggests accelerating Task B to minimize the overall impact on the timeline."
Optimization Algorithms	Suggests the most efficient resource allocation and scheduling strategies.	"AI reallocates tasks to maximize team productivity without exceeding the budget."
Automated Reporting	Generates progress reports and visualizations for stakeholders.	"AI creates a project dashboard highlighting completed tasks, risks, and budget usage."

Challenges and How AI Addresses Them

Challenge	How AI Helps	Example
Unclear Goals	AI assists in clarifying objectives using templates and best practices.	"ChatGPT suggests refining 'increase sales' to 'increase sales by 15% in 6 months through online campaigns.'"
Inaccurate Estimates	Uses historical data and predictive modeling to improve accuracy.	"AI estimates task duration based on past project data, reducing over-optimistic timelines."
Resource Constraints	Optimizes resource allocation to balance workloads and avoid bottlenecks.	"AI recommends assigning Task X to another team member to prevent burnout."
Changing Requirements	Provides flexibility by adapting plans dynamically with real-time data.	"AI updates the timeline and resource allocation after a major scope change."

Step-by-Step Example: AI in Action

Phase	Traditional Approach	AI-Enhanced Approach
Objective Setting	Stakeholders manually define vague goals.	AI refines objectives using stakeholder input and benchmarks: "Launch campaign to reach 1M users in 3 months."
Risk Analysis	Risks identified based on subjective judgment.	AI predicts high risk in digital ads due to low past performance, suggesting more investment in email marketing.
Resource Allocation	Team manually assigns tasks based on availability.	AI matches tasks with team members best suited for them based on skills, availability, and past success.
Schedule Optimization	Manual timelines lead to inefficiencies.	AI compresses timeline by scheduling overlapping tasks where possible without causing dependencies to fail.
Monitoring Progress	Requires manual status updates.	AI provides real-time updates: "Task A delayed by 1 day, suggest reallocating resource Y to maintain deadline."

Benefits of AI in Project Planning

Benefit	How It Transforms Planning
Increased Accuracy	Data-driven estimates reduce errors in timelines, budgets, and resource allocation.
Time Savings	Automates repetitive tasks like risk analysis and reporting, freeing time for strategic decisions.
Enhanced Collaboration	AI tools facilitate communication and transparency among stakeholders.
Proactive Risk Management	Predictive analytics identify potential risks before they escalate.
Better Decision-Making	Provides actionable insights based on real-time data and past trends.

Actionable Tips for AI-Driven Planning

1. **Start Small:** Integrate AI into one aspect of planning, such as scheduling or risk analysis, and expand as you gain confidence.

2. **Combine Human Judgment with AI Insights:** Use AI suggestions as a starting point but rely on team expertise for final decisions.
3. **Train Your Team:** Ensure your team understands how to interpret and act on AI-generated insights.
4. **Monitor AI Performance:** Regularly assess the effectiveness of AI tools and adjust algorithms or settings as needed.

Embrace AI as your planning partner. Start today by identifying one repetitive or data-intensive task in your project planning process that AI can enhance. Use the tools and strategies outlined here to take your project planning from good to great.

"AI is not the predictor; it is the guide—showing us possibilities, and helping us choose the right path forward."

-Ajay Tiwari

***

Chapter 4

The Shield Against Risks and the Gateway to Opportunities

"An ounce of prevention is worth a pound of cure."

- Benjamin Franklin

As Arjun was reviewing the latest project timelines for their autonomous driving initiative. Despite Maya's promising assistance with planning, something gnawed at him: risk. Could they anticipate and manage every variable in such a complex undertaking?

Krishna walked in, holding his ever-present tablet. "You look deep in thought, Arjun. Still wrestling with timelines?"

"No," Arjun replied, shaking his head. "It's the unknowns, the what-ifs. We've mapped the project well, but risks feel like shadows ready to pounce."

Krishna smiled knowingly and placed his tablet on the table. "You're about to meet the shield we've been working on. Maya isn't just a planner; she's the guard and our scout for opportunities. Let's see what she can do."

As Krishna activated Maya, her holographic form shimmered to life. "Good morning, Arjun," Maya said, her tone reassuring. "I understand you're concerned about risks. Let's discuss how I can help. But before we dive in, let's remember: every challenge has a hidden opportunity waiting to be discovered."

Arjun leaned forward. "I've managed risks before, Maya. But in this project, the stakes are too high. And opportunities? Frankly, we rarely talk about them. What makes you different from traditional tools?"

Maya's holographic display morphed into a dynamic risk and opportunity matrix. "Traditional tools rely on static inputs and often focus solely on risks. I analyze historical data, real-time variables, and probabilistic outcomes to manage risks and identify opportunities."

The hologram shifted to a past project's data a high-level automotive venture similar to their current one. "In this project," Maya began, "a delay in component deliveries triggered a domino effect, impacting timelines and budgets. Simultaneously, an overlooked process improvement opportunity could have saved weeks in production time."

The display zoomed in on a simulation where Maya predicted delays by correlating unusually high port traffic with supplier reports. She also highlighted an opportunity: leveraging AI-driven logistics optimization to expedite deliveries through alternative routes.

Krishna interjected, “Imagine having that kind of insight from day one. With Maya, we can move from reactive firefighting to proactive shielding and seize opportunities before they slip by.”

“Let’s turn to your project,” Maya suggested. “I’ve already processed the available data. Here’s what I found.”

The hologram transformed into a dashboard showing key risks and opportunities:

1. **Sensor Supply Chain Delays**: Global shortages of LiDAR, radar, and camera sensors could result in procurement delays, affecting development timelines.
2. **Regulatory Compliance Issues:** Autonomous vehicles must meet evolving safety and cybersecurity regulations, and gaps in documentation could delay approvals.
3. **Data Overload and System Lag:** Vehicles generate terabytes of data daily, leading to potential processing lags and delays in real-time decision-making.
4. **Team Resource Constraints and Burnout**: Highly specialized engineers and AI developers are in limited supply, leading to overwork and potential project slowdowns.
5. **Edge Case Scenarios in Autonomous Driving**: Uncommon road situations (e.g., unpredictable pedestrian behavior, extreme weather conditions) pose challenges for AI decision-making.
6. **Cybersecurity Threats**: Autonomous vehicles are vulnerable to hacking, data breaches, and potential manipulation of AI decision-making systems.
7. **Unexpected Hardware Failures**: Sensor malfunctions or calibration errors could lead to incorrect environmental perception, impacting safety.

8. **High Cost of Physical Testing**: Real-world testing is expensive and time-consuming, making it difficult to simulate every possible driving scenario.
9. **Market Adoption Uncertainty**: Public perception and trust in autonomous vehicles remain uncertain, affecting adoption rates and regulatory approvals.
10. **Legal and Liability Concerns**: Questions around accident liability, insurance claims, and legal accountability remain unresolved in many regions.

Then Maya suggested. "I've also processed the available data and found following opportunities."

1. **Supplier Diversification and Resilience**: Expanding partnerships with multiple sensor manufacturers could ensure a more stable supply chain.
2. **AI-Driven Testing Optimization**: Virtual simulations and AI-powered testing could reduce dependency on physical test runs, accelerating validation.
3. **Regulatory Expertise as a Competitive Advantage**: Investing in in-house regulatory specialists could position the company as a leader in compliance and certifications.
4. **Real-Time Data Insights for Predictive Maintenance**: AI-powered analytics could detect early signs of component failure, improving vehicle reliability.
5. **Fleet-Level AI Learning**: Connecting multiple autonomous vehicles to a shared learning system could improve collective decision-making and adaptability.
6. **Collaboration with Government and Research Institutions**: Partnering with regulatory bodies and universities could help shape industry standards and drive innovation.
7. **Monetization of AI Data**: Data collected from autonomous vehicles could be valuable for traffic optimization, smart city planning, and insurance models.

8. **Integration with Smart Infrastructure**: Collaborating with city planners to connect AVs with traffic signals and smart roads could enhance safety and efficiency.
9. **Consumer-Centric Features**: Developing personalized AI assistants and in-car experiences could differentiate the product in the competitive AV market.
10. **Sustainability and Energy Efficiency**: Enhancing energy-efficient AI models could reduce the carbon footprint of autonomous fleets.

Maya divided risks and opportunities into categories and provided strategies:

Risks	Description	Mitigation Strategies
Supply Chain Delays	Global shortages of LiDAR, radar, and camera sensors may cause procurement bottlenecks.	Establish backup suppliers and maintain buffer stock for critical components.
Regulatory Compliance Issues	Evolving regional laws or incomplete documentation may delay approvals.	Implement automated compliance tracking and engage early with regulators.
Data Overload	Large real-time sensor data can overwhelm processing units, leading to lags.	Optimize sensor configurations and implement edge computing for faster processing.
Resource Constraints	Limited AI engineers and hardware specialists may cause slowdowns or burnout.	Use dynamic resource allocation and introduce AI-assisted development tools.
Edge Case Scenarios	AI struggles with unpredictable pedestrian behavior, extreme weather, or rare traffic events.	Expand real-world testing and simulate edge cases using synthetic datasets.
Cybersecurity Threats	Autonomous systems are vulnerable to hacking, data breaches, and AI manipulation.	Implement end-to-end encryption, real-time intrusion detection, and robust security protocols.
Unexpected Hardware Failures	Sensor malfunctions or calibration errors can lead to faulty environmental perception.	Develop self-diagnostic mechanisms and establish predictive maintenance systems.

High Cost of Physical Testing	Real-world testing is expensive, making it hard to simulate every possible scenario.	Use digital twin simulations and virtual environments for scalable testing.
Market Adoption Uncertainty	Consumer trust and willingness to adopt autonomous technology remain unpredictable.	Conduct awareness campaigns, offer transparent safety reports, and introduce phased rollouts.
Legal and Liability Concerns	Questions remain on accident responsibility, insurance coverage, and accountability.	Collaborate with legal experts and insurers to define clear liability frameworks.

Opportunities and Actionable Strategies

Opportunities	Description	Actionable Strategies
Supplier Diversification	Reducing dependency on a single supplier can improve supply chain resilience.	Identify and establish contracts with alternative suppliers in different regions.
AI-Driven Testing Optimization	Automating routine testing can lower costs and improve validation accuracy.	Deploy AI-powered simulation environments and self-learning test cases.
Regulatory Expertise Building	In-house compliance experts can streamline future certifications.	Invest in regulatory training programs and create dedicated compliance teams.
Fleet-Level AI Learning	A shared learning system can improve decision-making across autonomous vehicles.	Develop cloud-based knowledge-sharing platforms for real-time data aggregation.
Government and Research Collaboration	Working with regulatory agencies and universities can shape industry standards.	Partner with research institutions and policymakers to contribute to regulatory frameworks.

Maya's tone grew gentle but firm, as if she were guiding them by the hand. "Every project comes with its own set of risks and opportunities," she began, her holographic form hovering beside a vibrant heat map. "The trick is not to chase every spark or extinguish every ember but to focus on what will move the needle the most." The heat map pulsed with color: deep reds marking the most critical threats, bright greens pinpointing the richest opportunities. Arjun leaned in as Maya spoke. "Notice here," she said, sweeping her finger over the map's top-left corner, "we have a high-impact, high-likelihood risk: supply chain delays. Because these delays can stall production and cascade into every subsequent phase, they demand our immediate attention."

Her finger glided to a vivid green patch in the bottom-right. "And here," she continued, "is a high-impact opportunity: AI-driven testing optimization. By automating and accelerating our test cycles, we can uncover defects earlier, shorten feedback loops, and even free up resources for more creative work."

Arjun exchanged a glance with Krishna, who nodded in agreement. Maya's display shifted to overlay a simple two-column chart: one side estimating the days and costs saved by addressing the testing opportunity first, the other showing the potential days lost and budget overrun if the supply chain risk went unchecked.

"Focus first on what matters most," Maya advised, her voice a calm anchor in the swirl of data. "If we mitigate the supply chain risk now securing alternative suppliers and adjusting inventory buffers, we protect our timeline. Simultaneously, investing in AI testing optimization will pay dividends in speed and quality. Together, these actions will reshape our project's trajectory."

As the heat map dimmed, the team felt a renewed clarity. They could see not only where trouble might strike, but also where they could leap ahead. With Maya's guidance, they were no longer adrift in uncertainty but steering toward their goals with purpose and precision.

Krishna loaded a real-world simulation into Maya. The hologram displayed a cyberattack on a vehicle's control system. Maya narrated, "The AI identified unusual data traffic patterns suggesting a breach. Immediate action isolated the compromised module, preventing further damage."

Simultaneously, Maya showed an opportunity from the same scenario: "Data from the breach allowed for improved algorithms, enhancing security protocols for future projects."

Krishna added, “Maya doesn’t just flag issues, she provides actionable solutions and uncovers silver linings.”

Arjun had one lingering doubt. “Maya’s impressive, but how do we ensure the team understands and trusts her outputs?”

Maya responded, “Communication is key. My reports are designed with clarity, featuring visual aids and actionable insights.” The hologram displayed a simplified dual report:

Risk	Opportunity
Regulatory Compliance Gap	Build regulatory expertise.
Impact: Delayed certifications	Impact: Long-term compliance advantage.
Recommended Actions: Automate checklists, consult regional experts.	Hire compliance professionals for scalability.

As the meeting wound down, Arjun’s skepticism had transformed into curiosity and respect. “These changes everything,” he said. “But implementing Maya isn’t just about tools, it’s about changing our mindset.”

Krishna nodded in agreement, his eyes reflecting the same quiet determination. “AI like Maya does more than automate tasks,” he said. “It gives us a dual advantage: shielding us from hidden risks while simultaneously uncovering opportunities we might otherwise miss. To harness this fully, we need to adopt a proactive mindset.”

Now, four guiding principles emerged:

1. Dual Approach

   Tackle risks directly while actively seeking and exploiting opportunities that can propel the project forward.

2. Prioritization

   Concentrate on those items with both high impact and high likelihood first, since they have the greatest potential to influence success.

3. Team Empowerment

   Translate Maya’s insights into clear, actionable steps so every team member understands what to do next and why it matters.

4. Culture Shift

   Foster an environment where proactive and innovative thinking becomes second nature, encouraging everyone to spot and act on risks or opportunities early.

Maya's journey from a simple analytics tool into a trusted team partner mirrored the transformation the team was undertaking. With her guidance, Arjun's group moved from reactive firefighting to strategic foresight.

To put these principles into practice, Maya outlined a five-step framework for managing risks and opportunities:

1. **Identify**

   Compile a comprehensive list of potential risks and opportunities through brainstorming sessions, AI-driven scans of historical data, and real time project feeds.

2. **Analyze**

   Plot each item on an impact versus probability matrix to determine which threats and prospects deserve immediate focus.

3. **Decide**

   Select the most suitable response for each priority item—whether that means mitigating, transferring, accepting, or exploiting it.

4. **Implement**

   Execute chosen actions swiftly and transparently, keeping all stakeholders informed and aligned on the plan.

5. **Monitor and Adapt**

   Treat the framework as a living document: continuously track how risks and opportunities evolve and adjust tactics as new information becomes available.

Armed with this roadmap and backed by Maya's ever watchful algorithms, the team was primed not just to navigate complexity but to transform every obstacle into a stepping stone toward success.

Summary

In this chapter, Arjun uncovered the dual power of Maya: not only as a risk manager but also as a scout for untapped opportunities. Through vivid examples, including a real-time demonstration, Maya showcases her ability to analyze historical data, monitor real-time variables, and use predictive analytics to foresee challenges and spot opportunities.

The chapter highlights a transformative shift from traditional reactive problem-solving to proactive risk and opportunity management, portraying Maya as a dynamic "shield" for the project team and a "key" unlocking new avenues of success.

SHIELD

- **S**pot Risks Early: Use AI to proactively detect risks before they escalate.
- **H**arness Data Insights: Leverage historical and real-time data for smarter decisions.
- **I**dentify Critical Issues: Pinpoint what matters most using prioritization tools.
- **E**valuate Impact and Likelihood: Focus on high-impact areas for effective planning.
- **L**everageAI Solutions:AdoptAI-driven recommendations to mitigate risks and seize opportunities.
- **D**rive Proactive Actions: Act decisively to shield your projects and unlock potential.

Use Appendix 8 to understand more in detail a step-by-step process to handle risks

Appendix 8: Empower Your Projects with AI

Arjun's integration of Maya into his team inspires a bold move towards smarter project management. Take the first steps to shield your own projects from risks and discover hidden opportunities:

1. **Spot Risks and Opportunities:** Review recurring challenges and potential wins in your past projects.
2. **Leverage AI:** Research and explore AI tools tailored for risk analysis and opportunity identification.
3. **Take Action Today:** Start small—implement one proactive strategy or AI-driven insight in your current project.

Your projects deserve both protection and growth. Make AI your ally, transforming how you manage risks and unlock opportunities for success.

Step-by-Step Guide to Identifying Risks and Solving Them

Risk identification is a critical aspect of project management, and with creative and innovative techniques, you can uncover hidden risks that traditional methods might overlook. Here's a step-by-step guide to identifying risks and effectively solving them:

Step 1: Start with a "Risk Radar" Workshop

Objective: Create an open, engaging environment where team members and stakeholders can brainstorm risks.

How	Tools	Example
Use a creative format like a "Risk Radar"	Divide risks into categories (e.g., technical, operational, market).	AI tools like Miro for brainstorming or ChatGPT to suggest risk categories.
Pose provocative questions	Ask, "What could go disastrously wrong?" or "What keeps you awake at night about this project?"	A team member identifies that reliance on a single supplier could delay deliveries.
Invite cross-functional inputs	Engage team members from diverse departments to get different perspectives.	Marketing raises concerns about customer acceptance of a new feature.

Step 2: Conduct "Scenario Storming"

Objective: Use creative scenarios to uncover risks that might not be immediately obvious.

How	Tools	Example
Simulate "What-If" scenarios	Ask AI to create plausible future events based on data trends.	"What if the competitor launches a similar product before us?"
Use predictive analytics	Leverage AI tools like IBM Watson or Tableau for trend analysis.	Predicts a spike in raw material costs due to market volatility.
Gamify the exercise	Create a risk board game where players score points by identifying potential project hurdles.	A participant highlights cybersecurity vulnerabilities during app development.

Step 3: Use AI-Enhanced Risk Detection

Objective: Let AI analyze data to identify hidden risks.

How	Tools	Example
Train AI on past projects	Feed historical data into AI to uncover recurring risks.	AI highlights that projects with aggressive deadlines often face quality issues.
Real-time risk monitoring	Integrate AI with project management tools to flag anomalies.	AI detects resource over-utilization early in the project phase.
Sentiment analysis	Use AI to assess team and stakeholder sentiments in emails or meetings to spot hidden concerns.	Negative sentiments about workload hint at burnout risk.

Step 4: Engage the "Invisible Stakeholder"

Objective: Consider risks from perspectives beyond your immediate stakeholders.

How	Tools	Example
Empathy mapping	Imagine how customers, regulators, or society at large could be impacted.	"What if the product's energy consumption violates new environmental laws?"
Cultural context analysis	Use AI to analyze regional, cultural, or demographic data for potential risks.	AI flags that a marketing strategy might not align with local cultural norms.
External advisors	Bring in industry experts to offer fresh perspectives on risks.	A legal consultant identifies potential data privacy compliance issues.

Step 5: Organize Risks in a Creative Framework

Objective: Make risks easier to analyze by categorizing them into a memorable, visual format.

Framework	How to Use It	Example
"Risk Tree"	Represent risks as branches stemming from root causes.	Root cause: "Supplier delays"; branches: "Material shortages," "Quality issues," etc.
"Iceberg Model"	Identify visible (obvious) risks above the surface and hidden (less apparent) risks below it.	Visible: "Scope changes"; Hidden: "Team miscommunication leading to rework."
RISK Acronym	Rank, Investigate, Solve, Keep tracking.	Use this to structure risk discussions during project meetings.

Step 6: Create Risk Profiles

Objective: Develop detailed profiles for each identified risk.

Profile Component	Details	Example
Risk Name	Give each risk a specific, descriptive title.	"Supply Chain Disruption"
Probability and Impact	Use AI to assign likelihood (low/ medium/high) and impact levels.	Probability: Medium; Impact: High.

Triggers	Identify events or conditions that might activate the risk.	Trigger: Supplier bankruptcy.
Mitigation Plan	Outline actions to reduce the risk's probability or impact.	Mitigation: Establish backup suppliers.

Step 7: Develop Action Plans for High-Priority Risks

Objective: Create actionable steps for preventing or responding to risks.

Plan Type	Details	Example
Preventive	Measures to avoid risk occurrence.	Sign contracts with two suppliers instead of one.
Contingency	Backup plans if the risk materializes.	Have an emergency budget allocated for unexpected costs.
Acceptance	Define how you will accept and live with certain low-impact risks.	Accept slight delays in delivery if costs are under control.

Step 8: Review and Reassess Continuously

Objective: Keep risks updated as the project evolves.

How	Tools	Example
Regular risk reviews	Schedule bi-weekly or monthly check-ins to revisit risks.	"Update: Cybersecurity risk has decreased due to recent system upgrades."
Real-time tracking dashboards	Use AI dashboards to monitor risks and mitigation efforts continuously.	AI dashboard shows that supplier delays are trending downward.
Feedback loops	Collect team and stakeholder feedback on how risks are evolving.	"Team feedback highlights new risks related to a subcontractor's work quality."

Creative Problem-Solving Steps

Once risks are identified, solving them requires a mix of traditional and innovative approaches.

Step	How to Solve	Example
1. Prioritize	Focus on high-probability, high-impact risks first.	Address "resource shortages" before tackling "minor delays in reporting."
2. Collaborate	Form cross-functional "risk response teams" to brainstorm solutions.	Team identifies that reusing existing modules can save time in case of delayed deliveries.
3. Leverage Technology	Use AI to model the effectiveness of various mitigation strategies.	AI shows that increasing buffer time reduces 80% of delay-related risks.
4. Test Solutions	Conduct simulations or small-scale pilots before full implementation.	Run a mock drill to test cybersecurity measures before deployment.
5. Communicate Transparently	Keep stakeholders informed about risks and mitigation strategies.	Share updates about how you're mitigating risks to boost confidence.

Proactive Risk Management Mindset

1. **Embrace Change:** Accept that risks evolve and require dynamic responses.
2. **Think Like a Futurist**: Anticipate trends that could impact your project.
3. **Cultivate Team Awareness**: Train your team to recognize and report risks early.
4. **Make AI Your Partner**: Use AI tools to amplify your ability to detect and respond to risks.

By following this creative and comprehensive approach, you can stay ahead of risks and ensure your project is on track for success.

Yes, there are several tools available to help identify, assess, and mitigate risks in projects effectively. These tools can enhance both manual and AI-driven risk management processes. Here's a categorized list:

Risk Identification Tools

Tool	Purpose	Features
MindMeister	Mind-mapping tool for brainstorming risks.	Collaborative maps, real-time editing, and visual brainstorming.
Miro	Visual collaboration platform for creating "Risk Radars."	Templates for risk analysis, brainstorming boards, and team collaboration.
Lucidchart	Diagramming tool for creating "Risk Trees" and "Iceberg Models."	Easy-to-use interface, integrations with other tools like Slack and Google Drive.
Stormboard	Brainstorming tool to categorize and visualize risks.	Sticky note format for visual risk clustering and idea management.

AI-Powered Risk Detection Tools

Tool	Purpose	Features
IBM Watson	Predictive analytics for identifying project risks.	Natural language processing, risk trend detection, and anomaly identification.
Microsoft Project with Copilot	AI-enhanced project planning and risk identification.	Task prioritization, budget predictions, and real-time risk flagging.
Google Looker	Business intelligence platform for trend and risk analysis.	AI-powered dashboards, data visualization, and predictive insights.
Tableau with Einstein Analytics	AI and data visualization for risk analysis and reporting.	Scenario modeling, predictive analysis, and automated risk reports.

Risk Assessment Tools

Tool	Purpose	Features
RiskWatch	Comprehensive tool for assessing and managing risks.	Compliance checks, risk scoring, and detailed reporting.
RiskyProject	Risk analysis and project planning.	Monte Carlo simulations, probability assessments, and integrated project scheduling.
Active Risk Manager (ARM)	Enterprise risk management software.	Risk dashboards, trend analysis, and detailed assessment matrices.
SpiraPlan	Project and risk management for software development.	Agile compatibility, test management, and integrated risk assessment.

Risk Tracking Tools

Tool	Purpose	Features
JIRA with Risk Management Plugins	Track risks throughout the project lifecycle.	Custom workflows, integration with development tools, and real-time tracking.
Smartsheet	Collaborative platform for tracking risks and tasks.	Gantt charts, real-time updates, and risk templates.
Monday.com	Task and risk tracking in agile and traditional projects.	Risk boards, automation, and easy reporting.
Asana	Manage project risks alongside tasks.	Risk templates, custom fields for probability/impact, and status tracking.

Simulation and Scenario Planning Tools

Tool	Purpose	Features
@Risk (by Palisade)	Monte Carlo simulations for risk scenarios.	Excel integration, probability distributions, and scenario modeling.
Deltek Acumen Risk	Simulation tool for risk and schedule analysis.	Identifies schedule weaknesses, evaluates mitigation options.
Oracle Primavera Risk Analysis	Scenario analysis and risk planning for large projects.	Predictive modeling, contingency planning, and quantitative risk analysis.

Communication and Reporting Tools

Tool	Purpose	Features
Slack with Risk Plugins	Communication platform with add-ons for tracking risks.	Risk alerts, team collaboration, and integration with project tools.
Power BI	Reporting tool for creating interactive dashboards.	Real-time data integration, AI-driven insights, and risk visualization.
Notion	Knowledge and task management tool.	Custom templates for risk registers, tracking, and mitigation plans.

General Project Management Tools with Risk Modules

Tool	Purpose	Features
Microsoft Project	End-to-end project planning with risk management features.	Timeline creation, risk flags, and integration with AI tools like Copilot.
Wrike	Task and risk management for cross-functional teams.	Risk logs, workflow automations, and custom dashboards.
ClickUp	Project and risk tracking.	Templates for risk management, real-time updates, and Gantt charts.

Example Use Cases

Scenario	Tool	How the Tool Helps
Identifying hidden risks in supply chain delays	IBM Watson	Analyzes historical data to flag supplier inconsistencies and potential disruptions.
Visualizing risk dependencies	Lucidchart	Creates "Risk Trees" showing how one risk might trigger another.
Mitigating risks with predictive insights	Tableau with Einstein Analytics	Simulates budget changes and predicts how they impact timelines.
Tracking risk mitigation progress	Monday.com	Provides a visual board for tracking each mitigation plan's status.

By combining these tools effectively, you can comprehensively address risks and enhance your project's resilience.

Risk Response Strategies

These strategies aim to minimize the likelihood or impact of a negative event.

Strategy	Description	Examples
Avoidance	Eliminate the risk entirely by changing the project plan or approach.	- Switch to a supplier with a proven track record to avoid delivery delays. - Avoid developing features with unstable technologies.
Reduction/ Mitigation	Reduce the likelihood or impact of the risk by proactive measures.	- Conduct extensive testing to mitigate software bugs. - Use predictive maintenance to prevent equipment failure.
Transfer	Shift the risk to a third party, such as an insurer or subcontractor.	- Purchase insurance for financial risks. - Outsource high-risk tasks to a specialized vendor.
Acceptance	Acknowledge the risk and plan to handle its impact if it occurs.	- Budget for potential delays. - Prepare a contingency fund for unexpected expenses.
Escalation	Pass the risk to higher management if it exceeds the project team's authority.	- Report major regulatory risks to the corporate legal team for expert handling.

Opportunity Response Strategies

These strategies aim to exploit or enhance the positive impacts of an opportunity.

Strategy	Description	Examples
Exploitation	Take direct action to ensure the opportunity is realized.	- Accelerate the launch of a product that meets high customer demand. - Fully adopt AI-driven solutions for resource optimization.
Enhancement	Increase the likelihood or impact of the opportunity.	- Improve marketing efforts for a successful campaign. - Upskill employees to handle emerging opportunities.
Sharing	Collaborate with external parties to maximize benefits.	- Partner with another organization to share resources and expertise for a joint project.
Acceptance	Take advantage of the opportunity if it happens but don't actively pursue it.	- Be prepared to scale production if demand unexpectedly increases.
Escalation	Pass the opportunity to higher management if it aligns better with strategic goals.	- Recommend executive leadership to invest additional funds in a high-growth market.

Risk & Opportunity Response Strategies in Action

Scenario	Type	Recommended Response Strategy
Sudden Regulatory Changes	Risk	**Avoidance**: Adjust the project scope to ensure compliance with new laws.
Emerging Market Trends	Opportunity	**Enhancement**: Allocate additional marketing budget to capitalize on the trend.
Supplier Delay	Risk	**Mitigation**: Diversify suppliers to reduce dependency.
Unexpected Skill Discovery	Opportunity	**Exploitation**: Assign skilled team members to critical tasks to boost efficiency.
Cybersecurity Vulnerability	Risk	**Transfer**: Hire a cybersecurity firm to handle data protection.

Unanticipated Funding Increase	Opportunity	**Sharing**: Partner with an R&D lab to explore innovative uses of funds.

"With AI as your shield, no risk is too big to manage, and no challenge too small to escape your notice."

— Ajay Tiwari

***

Chapter 5

The Collaborator: Teamwork in the AI Age

"Collaboration is not just about working together; it's about making each other better."

— Ajay Tiwari

The first light of dawn had barely crept into the room when Arjun's inbox pinged with urgency. A note from the sensor integration team warned of a sudden incompatibility between the LiDAR arrays and the onboard AI processor. He recognized this scenario all too well: one technical snag here could ripple out, delaying milestones and sapping his team's morale.

Moments later, Krishna appeared at the door and that familiar calm in his expression. "Looks like the day has started with a crisis," he observed, peering at Arjun's screen.

Arjun rubbed his temples. "It feels more like a wildfire. I need to tackle this immediately, yet I also have back-to-back strategy sessions today. How can I give both the attention they deserve?"

With a knowing smile, Krishna offered, "That is exactly why Maya is about to step in. Meet the collaborator."

When Krishna tapped his tablet, Maya's holographic image flickered into existence in the center of the conference room. Today her posture was relaxed but assured, radiating warmth.

"Good morning, Arjun," Maya greeted him. "I see you are facing an urgent integration challenge. Allow me to support your team."

Arjun leaned back in his chair, skepticism softening his tone. "I appreciate your help with risk assessment and planning, Maya. But fostering real collaboration among people that is an art."

Maya's digital features brightened as she replied, "Collaboration flourishes when human creativity meets structured support. My role is not to replace your team's synergy but to enhance it. Let me walk you through how I can weave myself into your workflows, smoothing communication, tracking progress, and suggesting adjustments so everyone remains aligned and empowered."

In that moment, Arjun sensed a shift. With Maya as collaborator, he could focus on strategy and leadership, confident that this new ally would keep the project moving forward, even though unexpected obstacles.

Maya quickly accessed the flagged issue in the project management system. The holographic display shifted to show a workflow of the sensor integration process, highlighting the problematic nodes.

"Here's the source of the issue," Maya explained. "It seems the LiDAR's firmware update conflicts with the processor's current configuration. I've already cross-referenced the specifications and identified a potential patch."

"That's impressive," Arjun admitted. "But who implements the fix?"

"I've assigned the task to Ravi, your lead engineer for hardware-software integration," Maya said. "He's the most qualified, and his schedule allows him to prioritize this immediately. I've also drafted a Slack message to update the rest of the team and ensure alignment. Shall I send it?"

"Go ahead," Arjun said, slightly awed.

Later that day, Arjun reviewed the updates Maya had facilitated. Ravi had already begun implementing the patch, and the team's Slack channel was abuzz with constructive discussions not the typical chaos Arjun was used to during crises.

"How did you manage to keep the communication so focused?" Arjun asked Maya during a feedback session.

Maya displayed a simplified communication map. "I analyze team interactions to identify optimal communication patterns. For example, in this instance, I noticed Ravi works best with direct updates rather than group discussions, so I tailored the message accordingly. At the same time, I kept others informed to avoid siloing information."

Arjun leaned back, impressed. "You've turned communication into an art form. But doesn't constant monitoring make people feel...watched?"

Krishna chimed in. "That's the beauty of it. Maya isn't intrusive. Her role is to guide, not to micromanage. Think of her as the ultimate facilitator, she ensures everyone has what they need to thrive."

Over the next week, Arjun observed how Maya seamlessly integrated into the team. She handled routine tasks like scheduling meetings, assigning responsibilities, and tracking deadlines. This freed up the team to focus on creative problem-solving and complex decision-making.

However, Arjun noticed something else: while Maya's efficiency was unparalleled, some team members seemed hesitant to fully engage with her.

"Not everyone trusts an AI collaborator," Arjun remarked to Krishna during a coffee break.

"That's natural," Krishna replied. "AI is a tool, not a replacement for human connection. The key is to balance automation with genuine interaction. You, as the leader, set the tone for that balance."

Taking Krishna's advice to heart, Arjun made an effort to connect personally with his team. He scheduled informal check-ins, praised individual contributions, and encouraged open discussions about Maya's role.

To his relief, these efforts bridged the gap. Team members began to see Maya not as a threat, but as a helpful assistant that complemented their skills.

A turning point came during a virtual stand-up meeting facilitated by Maya. Instead of the usual long, unstructured discussions, Maya provided a concise agenda based on each team member's current priorities.

"Let's start with Ravi," Maya began. "Your work on the LiDAR patch has reached 80% completion. Do you need any additional resources to finalize it?"

"Actually, yes," Ravi replied. "I need access to the latest processor specs to verify compatibility."

"I've already secured those specifications for you," Maya responded. "They're in your project folder."

The meeting continued in this streamlined manner, saving time and keeping everyone engaged.

Afterward, Arjun gathered feedback from the team. "What did you think of the meeting?" he asked.

"Efficient," Ravi replied. "It felt like we got straight to the point without losing focus."

"I agree," added Priya, the lead designer. "But I also appreciated how Maya highlighted individual contributions. It felt...personalized."

Another feature Maya introduced was a productivity dashboard. It showed team performance metrics without feeling invasive.

"How do you ensure this doesn't cross into micromanagement territory?" Arjun asked.

Maya's response was thoughtful. "Transparency and respect are crucial. My goal is not to monitor individuals but to identify patterns that help the team succeed. For example, I noticed a drop in productivity during late-afternoon meetings. Would you consider shifting them to mornings?"

Arjun nodded. "That's a fair observation. Let's try it."

Despite Maya's growing acceptance, a hiccup occurred when Ravi accidentally deleted a critical set of files while implementing the LiDAR patch.

"AI can't solve this," Ravi muttered, visibly frustrated.

"Actually, I can help," Maya interjected. "I've been backing up files in real-time. Would you like me to restore the previous version?"

The relief on Ravi's face was palpable. "Please do."

Within minutes, Maya had restored the files, and Ravi was back on track.

Later, Ravi approached Arjun. "I admit, I was skeptical about Maya. But today, she saved me hours of rework. She's like a safety net."

By the end of the quarter, the project was progressing smoothly. Maya's role as a collaborator had not only enhanced efficiency but also strengthened team dynamics.

"I never thought AI could be managing the day-to-day activities by being part of the team," Arjun said to Krishna during a wrap-up meeting.

"That's because Maya isn't just a tool," Krishna replied. "She's a partner in every sense of the word. And as you've seen, the real magic happens when human creativity and AI support work hand in hand."

Summary

In this chapter, Arjun and his team discover how Maya transforms teamwork in the AI age. From handling routine tasks to facilitating meaningful communication, Maya becomes a trusted collaborator. The story highlights the importance of balancing AI automation with genuine human connection, ensuring that technology enhances rather than replaces teamwork.

COLLABORATE

- **C**ommunicate Clearly
- **O**rganize Tasks Efficiently
- **L**everage AI Insights
- **L**isten to Team Feedback
- **A**djust Strategies as Needed
- **B**uild Trust Gradually
- **O**ptimize Resource Allocation
- **R**esolve Issues Proactively
- **A**cknowledge Individual Contributions
- **T**eamwork Over Technology
- **E**mpower Human Creativity

Ready to embrace AI as a collaborator? Start by identifying routine tasks that can be automated in your team. Explore AI tools that enhance communication and productivity. Remember to foster genuine human connections. Collaboration is the future and take the first step today! Utilize the Appendix 9 for handling the team effectively

Appendix 9: Team Dynamics: Understanding, Handling, and Motivating Your Team

Below is a table summarizing team dynamics, including types of team members, strategies for handling them, methods for measuring their contributions, identifying them, and fostering motivation. Additional points are included for enhancing overall team synergy. Make a table for your project for each project member.

Type of Team Member	How to Handle	How to Measure	How to Identify	How to Motivate	Addi-tional Notes
Leader	Empower with responsi-bilities; provide opportunities for decision-making.	Quality of decisions, team feedback, overall team perfor-mance.	Shows initiative, naturally takes charge, and inspires others.	Acknow-ledge their leadership; provide challen-ging tasks.	Leaders can mentor others to build team capacity.
Innovator	Encourage brain-storming and creative freedom; avoid microma-na-gement.	Number of ideas generated, successful implemen-tations.	Always brings fresh ideas, challenges the status quo.	Recognize their ideas publicly and provide time/ resources for experime-ntation.	Ensure their ideas align with project goals.
Analyzer	Provide clear data and objectives; ensure structured commu-nication.	Accuracy of analysis, relevance of insights.	Thrives on data, prefers logical discussions over emotional arguments.	Provide access to tools for analysis and reward their precision.	Use their skills in risk assess-ment and problem-solving.
Executor	Set clear goals and deadlines; ensure consistent commu-nication.	Task completion rate, timeliness, and quality of work.	Prefers defined tasks, shows reliability in execution.	Celebrate achieve-ments and provide clear next steps.	Pair them with leaders for better align-ment.

Collabo-rator	Foster teamwork; use them to bridge gaps between team members.	Feedback from peers, conflict resolution effective-ness.	Excels in mediating conflicts and building relation-ships.	Highlight their role in team cohesion and reward inclusivity.	Use them in cross-functional tasks.
Critic	Encourage constructive feedback; channel criticism positively.	Quality of feedback, impact on team decisions.	Always points out flaws and potential pitfalls.	Show how their feedback leads to improve-ments; involve them in solution-building.	Balance criticism with positive reinforce-ment to avoid negativity.
Quiet Contri-butor	Create a safe space for ideas; actively involve them in discussions.	Quality of contribu-tions, engage-ment in meetings.	Reserved but often delivers deep insights when asked.	Value their input and provide time to think before respon-ding.	Use one-on-one discu-ssions to under-stand their perspe-ctive.
Visionary	Align their ideas with long-term goals; keep them grounded in practicality.	Future-oriented ideas, alignment with project vision.	Talks about long-term impacts and sees the “big picture.”	Provide platforms to discuss and refine their visions.	Combine their vision with the innova-tor’s creativity and analyzer’s logic.
Optimist	Leverage their positivity during challenging times; ensure realistic expectations.	Team morale during challenges, problem-solving approach.	Brings energy and enthusiasm to the group.	Celebrate their ability to uplift the team and involve them in team-building activities.	Encou-rage them to help tackle low-motivation periods.
Realist	Balance optimism with realism; involve them in planning stages.	Accuracy of predictions, alignment with project outcomes.	Always provides practical solutions and warns about potential issues.	Acknow-ledge their practicality and show how it benefits the project.	Pair with optimists to strike a balance.

Key Points to Enhance Team Synergy

1. **Foster Diversity**: Encourage diverse skills, perspectives, and approaches to problem-solving.
2. **Clear Roles and Responsibilities**: Ensure everyone knows their specific role and how it ties to the bigger picture.
3. **Open Communication**: Use regular meetings and feedback sessions to maintain transparency and resolve conflicts.
4. **AI Tools for Analysis**: Leverage tools like Microsoft Teams, Trello, or AI-based sentiment analysis tools to understand team dynamics and workload balance.
5. **Personal Development Plans**: Align team roles with individual career aspirations to ensure personal and organizational growth.
6. **Recognition and Rewards**: Recognize contributions both privately and publicly to maintain morale and motivation.

Dynamic Role and Responsibility Management Table

Aspect	What to Do	Example	Tool/ Technique	Why It Works
Understand the Current Landscape	Identify team strengths and project needs.	Map tasks for a delayed product launch using a skills matrix.	SWOT Analysis, Skills Matrix	Helps assign roles based on expertise.
Define Core Responsi-bilities	Specify stable tasks and include flexibility for evolving needs.	"Content Specialist writes blogs + supports new campaigns."	RACI Matrix	Creates clarity even in dynamic scenarios.

Collaborate with the Team	Involve team members in defining roles for adaptability.	Developers suggest pairing QA tasks with coding reviews.	Team Brainsto-rming	Ensures buy-in and fosters ownership.
Commu-nicate Changes Frequently	Use daily/ weekly updates to align roles dynami-cally.	Marketing Lead shifts to prioritize a new product launch.	Daily Standups, Dynamic Dashboards	Reduces confusion during rapid changes.
Document and Track Changes	Maintain a shared, real-time updated role document.	Update Trello cards with role revisions after a meeting.	Google Docs, Trello	Prevents miscommunication or role overlap.
Escalation Protocols	Set clear decision-making chains for conflicts or overlaps.	"UI design disputes escalated to Project Manager."	Clear Org Chart, Playbooks	Prevents delays during dynamic shifts.
Monitor Role Effective-ness	Use feedback and task completion rates to refine roles.	"Sales Rep feedback leads to splitting customer calls by priority."	Surveys, Perfor-mance Metrics	Ensures changes enhance team efficiency.
Foster Adapta-bility	Encourage learning new skills and embracing flexibility.	Designers learn basic video editing for faster turnarounds.	Online Courses, Mentorship	Builds resilience in a changing environment.

Example Scenario: Mid-Project Scope Shift

Initial Scope: Develop a marketing campaign.
Change: Add live event management.

1. **What Changed?** Event planning added, straining the existing team.
2. **Solution**: Reassign roles:
   - Marketing Lead → Coordinate event logistics.
   - Content Writer → Create live scripts and promotional materials.
   - Graphic Designer → Design event banners and visuals.
3. **Outcome**: Realignment documented in a Trello board, ensuring clarity.

By staying agile, dynamic changes become opportunities for growth, not chaos.

"In the AI age, collaboration isn't just human-to-human; it's human-to-AI, creating a synergy that drives success."

— Ajay Tiwari

***

Chapter 6

Eyes in the Sky: Real-Time Project Monitoring

"Success in project management doesn't come from having all the answers but from knowing where to look."

-Ajay Tiwari

It was 8 months into the project, Arjun was on top of the project with Maya's assistance but there was something bothering him. The ADAS project was in a critical phase. Deadlines loomed like storm clouds, and the slightest misstep could derail months of effort.

At precisely 11:57 PM, Maya's notification chimed.

"Subject: Critical Alert – Budget Utilization Spike in Sensor Calibration Phase."

Arjun's eyes widened. A spike? At this hour? Opening the email, he saw Maya's report, neatly summarized. The calibration sub team had consumed 15% more budget than planned in the past week.

Arjun called Krishna. "Maya's flagged a potential issue. Calibration costs are spiraling. What do you make of it?"

Krishna chuckled groggily on the other end. "Looks like Maya's kicked into 'eyes in the sky' mode. She's monitoring every detail, real-time. Let's dive in tomorrow morning."

The next day, the project team gathered in the conference room. Maya's holographic form appeared in front of them, this time with a dynamic dashboard displaying graphs, alerts, and key metrics.

"Good morning, everyone," Maya began. "Let's review the state of the project."

The room hushed as Maya outlined the flagged issue. "Sensor calibration costs have exceeded projections due to overtime hours and unexpected equipment wear. I've identified the equipment anomalies contributing to the overages and flagged vendor invoices for further review."

Priya, the lead designer, leaned forward. "How did you even notice this in time? These kinds of discrepancies often slip through until the next budget review."

Maya's display zoomed out, showing the interconnected elements of the project plan. "I continuously monitor real-time data across all subprojects. When patterns deviate significantly from baselines, I analyze and prioritize potential impacts. This ensures early detection."

Over the next week, Maya's role as a real-time overseer became more evident. She tracked everything from team progress and milestone adherence to budget flows and resource utilization.

In one instance, Maya noticed a lag in the prototyping phase. "The 3D printing team is two days behind schedule," she informed Arjun during the daily check-in. "The delay stems from supply chain bottlenecks. I recommend reallocating materials from a lower-priority phase to keep the critical path intact."

Krishna mentioned in agreement. "This kind of proactive adjustment would've taken days for you to realize on our own."

"Exactly," Maya said. "By maintaining a bird's-eye view, I provide insights that help you adapt in real-time, minimizing disruptions."

One of Maya's most impressive feats was her ability to identify trends invisible to the human eye.

During a weekly review, she displayed an intriguing correlation. "I've observed a pattern where productivity spikes on Wednesdays but dips on Fridays. Additionally, tasks requiring cross-team collaboration tend to see delays in approvals."

Ravi frowned. "I knew Fridays were slower, but I hadn't connected it to collaboration. What's causing the bottleneck?"

Maya highlighted communication logs. "Cross-team requests are often submitted late in the week, leading to delays as teams prioritize their own end-of-week tasks. A simple adjustment to request submission timelines could resolve this."

Arjun made a note. "Let's implement that change immediately. These insights are gold."

Despite Maya's accuracy, her omnipresent oversight occasionally sparked unease.

"I feel like every move we make is under a microscope," Ravi admitted during a coffee break. "It's helpful, sure, but it's also... intense."

Arjun empathized. "I get it. But remember, Maya's not here to judge. She's here to support us. Think of her as the ultimate safety net, not a watchdog."

To ease the team's concerns, Arjun held a workshop where Maya demonstrated her monitoring process transparently. She explained how data was anonymized where possible and how her focus was on trends, not individuals.

By the end of the session, Ravi spoke up. "That clears up a lot. It's not about micromanaging it's about seeing the big picture."

It was a typical Friday evening. The hum of computers softened as team members packed up for the weekend, the atmosphere tinged with a sense of accomplishment. But just as Arjun reached for his bag, Maya's alert system came alive, flashing an ominous red.

"Critical Alert: Delay Detected in Testing Phase – Delivery Timeline at Risk."

The room froze. Arjun's heart raced as he leaned forward, his voice sharp. "What's going on, Maya?"

Maya's calm and composed holographic figure illuminated the dimming room. "The testing environment has encountered a compatibility issue with the new firmware. If unresolved, this delay could cascade into subsequent phases, jeopardizing the delivery schedule," she reported.

Arjun's face tightened. "How bad is it?"

"Critical," Maya replied. "However, I've analyzed the scenario and identified a viable workaround. The testing lead has already been alerted and is reviewing the proposed solution."

Krishna, who had just walked in with his tablet, listened intently. "This issue could've easily gone unnoticed until Monday, causing a domino effect across the timeline," he remarked. "Instead, we're tackling it now. That's the power of Maya."

The team gathered quickly, rallying around Maya's suggested plan. The workaround involved a temporary modification to the test parameters, enabling progress while the compatibility issue was being resolved in parallel. Clear instructions from Maya made execution swift and seamless.

Within hours, the issue was mitigated, and the testing phase resumed without compromising the project schedule. Arjun exhaled a sigh of relief, his gratitude evident. "We could've lost weeks fixing this. Instead, we've contained it before it even became a problem."

Krishna nodded. "This is what proactive risk management looks like. Maya didn't just identify the issue—she gave us the tools and foresight to address it immediately."

As the team dispersed, Arjun reflected on the moment. Maya wasn't just an assistant; she was becoming an indispensable part of their operation a guardian against chaos and a beacon of solutions when everything seemed on the brink of falling apart.

As the project progressed, Maya's real-time monitoring became an indispensable part of the workflow. The team no longer saw her as just an AI tool they saw her as an invaluable overseer, constantly scanning the horizon for potential issues.

One day, Priya approached Arjun. "You know, I never thought I'd say this, but I can't imagine running a project without Maya. She's like the ultimate project guardian."

Arjun smiled. "She's definitely changed the game. But the real credit goes to the team—you've embraced this new way of working with open minds."

Summary

This chapter showcased how Maya transformed into the ultimate overseer, providing real-time monitoring that kept the ADAS project on track. By tracking milestones, budgets, and team progress, Maya helped the team catch potential issues before they escalated. She also uncovered hidden trends, enabling proactive adjustments.

SKY

- **S**can Continuously: Use AI to monitor all project aspects in real-time.
- **K**now Trends: Identify patterns and correlations that inform decision-making.
- **Y**ield Early Insights: Act on alerts before issues spiral out of control.

Call to Action

Start leveraging AI tools to keep an eye on your projects. Set up real-time monitoring systems, and trust the insights they provide to adapt proactively. Let AI be your eyes in the sky, ensuring no detail goes unnoticed!

Appendix 10: Methods to Leverage AI for Project Monitoring

Method	Description	Example Tool/ Technique	Expected Outcome
Identify Suitable AI Tools	Research and select AI tools tailored to project monitoring.	Tools like **Azure Boards, Jira AI**, **Asana Intelligence**, or **Monday.com AI**.	Enhanced tracking and reporting of project milestones.
Integrate AI with PM Platforms	Connect AI tools with existing project management software to streamline data flow.	Use AI-powered add-ons like **Microsoft CoPilot** in Microsoft Teams.	Centralized real-time updates and predictive insights.
Set Up Real-Time Dashboards	Establish interactive dashboards for tracking tasks, timelines, and risks dynamically.	Dashboards in **Power BI** or **Tableau** with AI plugins.	Instant visibility into project status and potential risks.
Automate Notifications	Configure alerts for critical metrics or deviations from project plans.	Use AI bots like **Azure Workflow, Slack Workflow AI** for automated alerts.	Prompt action on issues before they escalate.

Conduct Historical Data Analysis	Train AI with past project data to identify patterns and predict future risks.	Tools like **Google Vertex AI** for analyzing trends.	Better forecasting and preemptive issue mitigation.
Adopt Predictive Analytics	Use AI to predict delays, resource shortages, or budget overruns.	Leverage tools like **Crystal AI** or **Smartsheet Predictive Analytics**.	Increased accuracy in project planning and resource allocation.
Facilitate Team Training	Ensure the team understands how to interpret and act on AI insights.	Host workshops or provide tutorials on **AI-enabled tools**.	Improved collaboration and faster decision-making.
Simulate Scenarios	Test AI's capabilities in hypothetical project scenarios to understand its value.	Run simulations in **Autodesk Forge** or **Digital Twins AI**.	Confidence in leveraging AI during live projects.
Review AI Recommen-dations Regularly	Periodically evaluate the effectiveness of AI's suggestions and refine settings.	Schedule weekly reviews with AI-generated reports.	Continuous improvement and trust in AI insights.

Real life examples where AI can assist.

1. Vendor Delays in Procurement

Scenario:

I was managing a project where a key vendor delayed delivering critical components, risking the entire production schedule.

AI Solution:

- AI tools like tickets & Microsoft Power BI flagged inconsistencies in the vendor's historical delivery data and correlated them with external market trends.
- It suggested alternate vendors with better on-time delivery records.
- Predictive analytics helped the team negotiate revised terms with the current vendor and secure a backup supplier.

Outcome:

The project stayed on track with minimal disruption, and the team avoided costly downtime.

2. **Overworked Team Members**

Scenario:

During an intense development phase, some team members began missing deadlines due to burnout, which affected the project's momentum.

AI Solution:

- AI such as Workday Peakon detected patterns of overwork through project tracking data and team sentiment surveys.
- It recommended reallocating tasks, automating repetitive activities, and adjusting timelines for non-critical deliverables.
- A dynamic workload distribution system was implemented to balance the team's efforts.

Outcome:

The team's morale improved, and the project resumed its pace without sacrificing quality.

3. **Misalignment in Regulatory Documentation**

Scenario:

While working on an ADAS project, regulatory documentation was flagged for non-compliance in certain regions late in the project timeline.

AI Solution:

- Tools like DocuSign AI scanned all project documents and highlighted gaps in compliance requirements.
- It cross-referenced regional regulations and provided recommendations to update documentation.
- Automated workflows ensured the changes were quickly approved and disseminated to stakeholders.

Outcome:

The project passed regulatory audits smoothly, avoiding penalties and delays.

4. Sudden Testing Failures

Scenario:

Midway through software testing, a critical compatibility issue arose between the new firmware and the existing hardware, jeopardizing the delivery timeline.

AI Solution:

- Maya (AI tool) flagged this issue by analyzing test logs and system telemetry in real-time.
- It suggested reconfiguring the firmware setup and isolating non-critical tests to expedite the process.
- A workaround was implemented to maintain progress while resolving the core issue in parallel.

Outcome:

The testing schedule stayed intact, and the delivery deadline was met successfully.

5. Budget Overshooting During Execution

Scenario:

In one of my projects, resource costs unexpectedly escalated, causing the budget to overrun halfway through the execution phase.

AI Solution:

- Jira AI tracked resource allocations and flagged deviations from the approved budget in real time.
- AI-driven cost-optimization strategies suggested alternatives, such as shifting to a more affordable cloud provider and renegotiating vendor contracts.
- Predictive analysis identified areas where costs could be trimmed without affecting deliverables.

Outcome:

The project got completed within the revised budget, with lessons applied for future financial planning.

These examples highlight how AI tools help tackle real challenges, offering actionable insights and proactive solutions to manage risks, optimize resources, and ensure project success.

"AI gives you eyes in the sky, offering a perspective that sees everything and misses nothing."

— Ajay Tiwari

***

Chapter 7

The Decision Engine

"In the end, it is not the data that makes the decision, but the wisdom to interpret it."

— Ajay Tiwari

The ADAS project had reached a pivotal juncture. The team was preparing for the final integration phase, and two possible paths lay ahead. The first was a streamlined approach that promised faster delivery but relied on untested modules. The second was a more cautious route, requiring thorough testing but risking delays.

As the team debated the merits of each approach, Maya sent a notification to Arjun. **"Decision Point Analysis Ready: Two Options Evaluated Based on Project Priorities."**

Arjun paused the discussion. "Let's see what Maya has to say before we proceed."

The team gathered around the central display as Maya appeared, her holographic presence exuding calm authority.

"Good afternoon, team," she began. "I've analyzed both scenarios, factoring in timelines, resource availability, risk tolerance, and project goals. Let's explore the insights together."

Maya's holographic interface transitioned into a sleek, compressed timeline. The adjusted schedule aimed for an ambitious 12% reduction in delivery time.

Maya's Analysis:

"This streamlined approach accelerates the project by eliminating certain testing redundancies and parallelizing tasks. However, it introduces a 35% likelihood of encountering integration issues due to the untested modules."

The room fell silent as Maya detailed the potential trade-offs.

- **Impact of Integration Issues:**
  - If encountered, these issues could cascade through the system, requiring an additional two weeks to resolve.
  - This delay could nullify the initial time savings and increase budget consumption by 7%.
- **Team Dynamics:**
  - The high-pressure timeline would push the team to its limits, risking burnout and reduced efficiency.

Arjun asked, "Can we mitigate these risks?"

Maya's display adjusted, introducing potential mitigation strategies.

1. **Reprioritize Tasks:**
   - Shift non-critical tasks to later phases, freeing resources for immediate priorities.

2. **Increase Resources:**
   - Allocate additional personnel or tools to test the high-risk modules.
   - Downside: This stretches team bandwidth and could increase costs by an additional 3%.

Conclusion:

While the streamlined approach offered a faster delivery, it posed significant risks to integration quality, team morale, and budget stability.

Maya's interface shifted again, this time to a slower but more thorough timeline. The cautious approach extended the project by 10 days.

Maya's Analysis:

"This approach includes comprehensive testing for all modules. It minimizes integration risks to under 10%, ensuring a 95% likelihood of delivering a fully functional product within the extended timeline."

Key Factors:

- **Risk Minimization:**
  - By allowing more time for rigorous testing, the approach drastically reduces the chances of encountering unexpected issues during deployment.

- **Client Prioritization:**
  - Maya analyzed past client communications and project priority weighting. "The client prioritizes reliability over speed. A premature delivery with

potential functionality gaps could negatively impact satisfaction and future collaboration."

Priya asked, "But the client has expressed urgency for faster delivery. How would they perceive the delay?"

Maya's Insight:

The display transitioned to a sentiment analysis:

1. **Historical Patterns:**
   - In previous projects, the client showed a preference for quality, even at the cost of minor delays.
2. **Reputation Impact:**
   - Delivering a reliable product strengthens client trust, while an early delivery with defects risks damaging the relationship.
3. **Team Benefits:**
   - The cautious approach also supported the team's well-being by maintaining a balanced workload, reducing stress, and avoiding late-phase firefighting.

Summary of Choices

Aspect	Streamlined Approach	Cautious Approach
Timeline	Reduced by 12%, but at risk of 2-week setbacks.	Extended by 10 days.
Risk of Integration Issues	High (35%).	Low (under 10%).
Budget Impact	+7% with risk of +3% for mitigations.	Minimal impact.
Client Sentiment	Risk of dissatisfaction due to potential defects.	High likelihood of trust and satisfaction.
Team Dynamics	Increased stress and potential burnout.	Balanced workload and morale.
Suitability	For urgent, low-complexity projects.	For complex, reliability-critical projects.

The room buzzed with discussion. Maya's analysis was thorough, but the final decision required human judgment.

Arjun turned to his team. "Maya's given us incredible insights, but it's up to us to make the call. What do we prioritize—speed or stability?"

Krishna spoke first. "I think we should prioritize stability. The ADAS system is safety-critical. A rushed integration with errors could undermine the project's reputation."

Priya nodded. "I agree. But we should also communicate transparently with the client, showing them why the cautious approach serves their long-term interests better."

Arjun looked at Maya. "What would the cautious path mean for resource allocation?"

Maya adjusted her display. "You'd need to extend contractor engagements by a week and reallocate 15% of current resources to testing. The budget impact would be marginal, as the additional time offsets overtime costs."

With the room in agreement, Arjun made the call. "Let's proceed with the cautious approach. Maya, draft a revised timeline and prepare a client communication plan."

Over the next few weeks, the team worked on the revised plan. Maya's role shifted to facilitating the adjusted timeline and ensuring the additional testing was efficient.

One evening, Priya reflected on the process. "You know, it's amazing how Maya doesn't just spit out answers. She gives us the tools to make smarter decisions ourselves."

Krishna nodded. "Yeah, it's like she's the engine, but we're still the drivers."

Case Study: A Smarter, Faster Decision

The integration phase wasn't the first time Maya had played a critical role in decision-making. Earlier in the project, the team faced a dilemma about sensor procurement.

Two vendors had bid for the contract: one offered lower costs but longer delivery times, while the other promised quicker delivery at a premium.

Maya had analyzed the bids, considering factors such as vendor reliability, potential delays, and the project's critical path. She presented a weighted score for each vendor, highlighting that the premium vendor's reliability historically reduced rework, saving time and costs in the long run.

The team chose the premium vendor based on Maya's insights, and the decision paid off when the sensors arrived ahead of schedule, enabling an early start to testing.

Not every decision was as clear-cut. During a brainstorming session about user interface design, Maya's recommendation clashed with Priya's creative instincts.

Maya had suggested a minimalist design based on user feedback trends. Priya, however, felt the design lacked warmth and personality.

"Your data is solid, Maya," Priya said, "but sometimes creativity isn't about trends, it's about standing out."

Arjun encouraged a balanced approach. "What if we use Maya's insights as a baseline but infuse Priya's creative vision into the final design?"

The result was a unique interface that resonated with users while aligning with their preferences—a testament to the power of blending AI-driven insights with human creativity.

By the end of the project, Maya had become more than just a tool. She was a trusted partner, helping the team navigate complex decisions with clarity and confidence.

Krishna summed it up during the final team debrief. "Maya's not just about making decisions faster—it's about making them better. And she reminds us that the best decisions happen when data and experience work together."

Summary

This chapter highlighted how Maya empowered the ADAS project team to make smarter, faster decisions. From analyzing complex trade-offs to balancing data with intuition, Maya acted as the ultimate decision engine, driving clarity and confidence.

ENGINE

- **E**valuate Options: Use AI to analyze all possible paths.
- **N**eutral Analysis: Rely on AI's objective insights for clarity.
- **G**uide with Data: Let AI provide a foundation for decisions.
- **I**ntegrate Expertise: Pair AI insights with human judgment.
- **N**avigate Complexity: Leverage AI for multidimensional decisions.
- **E**nhance Outcomes: Achieve smarter, faster, and more reliable decisions.

Call to Action

Embrace AI as your decision engine. Trust its insights, but always blend them with your expertise and intuition. Together, you and AI can navigate even the most complex decision points with clarity and confidence!

Step-by-Step Guide to Embrace AI as Your Decision Engine

1. **Understand AI's Role:**

Recognize that AI doesn't replace your expertise but complements it by providing data-driven insights and predictions.

Example:

In a software development project, AI tools like GitHub Copilot assist in code generation and bug detection. However, your judgment ensures the generated code aligns with project requirements and quality standards.

2. **Set Clear Goals:**

Define the objectives you want AI to help achieve—whether it's optimizing timelines, mitigating risks, or streamlining resource allocation.

Example:

For a marketing campaign, AI can analyze customer data to suggest optimal ad placement strategies. Your expertise ensures the strategy resonates with the brand's voice and target audience.

3. **Integrate AI in Decision-Making Processes:**

Use AI tools to analyze scenarios, model outcomes, and offer actionable recommendations.

Example:

While launching a product, an AI tool forecasts potential market responses based on past data. It might suggest targeting specific demographics with aggressive pricing. You can adjust the pricing strategy considering cultural nuances and competitor positioning.

4. **Blend Insights with Intuition:**

Trust AI's data but validate it with your domain knowledge and experience.

- Use AI insights to identify trends or anomalies.
- Apply your expertise to interpret and act on those insights.

Example:

During a supply chain project, AI flags a potential delay due to weather conditions. Based on your knowledge of local suppliers, you decide to source from an alternative vendor AI hadn't prioritized, ensuring smoother operations.

5. Pilot AI Recommendations Before Full Implementation:

Test AI's insights on a smaller scale to evaluate effectiveness before scaling up.

Example:

AI suggests automating a manufacturing process to save costs. You run a pilot on one production line to measure impact and efficiency before rolling it out plant-wide.

6. Foster a Collaborative AI-Human Culture:

Train your team to trust and use AI insights while encouraging critical thinking.

Example:

In a customer service department, an AI system prioritizes support tickets. Agents are trained to understand why certain tickets are flagged as high-priority and make final decisions on escalation based on contextual nuances.

Real-World Applications and Success Stories

Scenario	AI Contribution	Human Expertise Added
Autonomous Driving Development	AI predicts risks from supplier delays and suggests buffer stocks.	Team decides to also establish a local supplier base to counter international shipping risks.
Financial Planning	AI identifies investment patterns and suggests portfolio adjustments.	Portfolio manager refines choices based on geopolitical events and specific client goals.
Healthcare Diagnosis	AI analyzes patient data to identify potential conditions.	Doctor cross-checks findings with patient history and symptoms before making a final diagnosis.
Retail Inventory Management	AI recommends stocking trends based on purchase data and seasonality.	Retailer adjusts based on local events (e.g., festivals or sporting events).
Construction Project Scheduling	AI proposes an optimized schedule based on resource availability and weather forecasts.	Project manager integrates local labor union schedules and festival holidays into the plan.

By combining the analytical precision of AI with human creativity and judgment, decision-making becomes more robust. Just as a pilot trusts their instruments but navigates storms with experience, you can let AI illuminate the path while steering your project with intuition. Together, this partnership transforms uncertainty into clarity and confidence.

"AI helps you make decisions faster, smarter, and with more insight than ever before, but the final call still rests with you."

— Ajay Tiwari

***

Chapter 8

The Taskmaster: Automation Unleashed

"Automation is not about replacing people; it's about liberating them to do more meaningful work."

— Ajay Tiwari

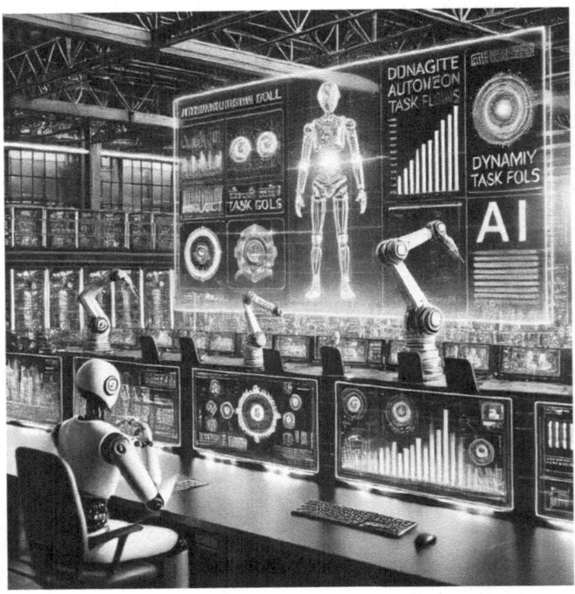

It was a crisp Monday morning, and Arjun arrived at his desk with a sense of determination. The ADAS project was on track, but his personal workload felt like a never-ending wave. Endless status reports, task allocations, and follow-up emails had consumed his time, leaving little room for strategy or innovation.

He glanced at Maya, who seemed to sense his frustration. **"Good morning, Arjun. Would you like assistance in optimizing today's workload?"**

Arjun chuckled. "More like saving me from drowning in it, Maya."

Maya's interface sprang to life. "Let's delegate repetitive tasks to me. I'll free up your time for higher-value work."

Maya's proposition wasn't new. For months, she had been assisting the team with predictive analytics and decision-making, but now she offered to take on routine administrative tasks. Arjun was hesitant.

"Won't automation make me lose oversight?" he asked.

Maya's response was reassuring. "Automation is not about relinquishing control. It's about empowering you to focus on strategic priorities while I handle repetitive tasks. You'll remain in the loop with real-time updates."

Arjun decided to take the plunge. "Okay, Maya. Let's see what you've got."

Maya began by analyzing Arjun's daily activities.

"Here are tasks I recommend automating," she said, displaying a categorized list:

1. **Status Reporting**: Collecting and formatting progress data for weekly reports.
2. **Task Allocation**: Assigning routine tasks based on team member availability and expertise.
3. **Meeting Scheduling**: Coordinating calendars to find optimal meeting times.
4. **Follow-Up Reminders**: Sending gentle nudges for overdue tasks.

Arjun raised an eyebrow. “All of that? Are you sure?”

Maya nodded. “These tasks consume 35% of your workweek. Automating them will save approximately 12 hours per week.”

The first task Maya tackled was status reporting. She integrated with the team’s tools, pulling real-time data on milestones, resource utilization, and risk metrics.

By noon, Maya presented a polished report to Arjun. “Here’s the status update for today. Would you like to review or share it directly?”

Arjun reviewed the report. It was detailed, clear, and formatted perfectly. He clicked “Send,” and the report was instantly distributed to stakeholders.

Next, Maya took over task allocation. Based on a backlog of pending assignments, she matched tasks to team members using a combination of skill sets, workload distribution, and deadlines.

“Maya, this is incredible,” Priya said later that day. “It’s like you’ve lifted a huge weight off our shoulders.”

While automation was a game-changer, it wasn’t without its hiccups.

During one task allocation, Maya assigned Krishna to a coding task better suited for another team member.

“Why did Maya assign this to me?” Krishna asked Arjun.

Arjun investigated and found that Maya had prioritized Krishna’s availability over expertise.

“Maya, let’s refine the algorithm,” Arjun said. “Include skill proficiency as a higher priority when assigning tasks.”

Maya adjusted instantly. “The task allocation model has been updated. Thank you for your feedback.”

This incident taught the team an important lesson: automation is a partnership. Continuous fine-tuning ensures optimal results.

With automation taking over mundane tasks, Arjun’s schedule opened up. He used the newfound time to brainstorm innovative features for the ADAS system.

During a creative session, he proposed a driver-assistance mode for cyclists, inspired by a recent road trip. The idea sparked excitement among the team.

"Without Maya handling the busywork, I wouldn't have had the bandwidth to think about this," Arjun admitted.

Balancing Automation and Oversight

As Maya's capabilities expanded, Priya raised a valid concern. "How do we ensure we're still in control? Automation is great, but we can't let it replace human judgment."

Maya addressed the team. "Automation complements your expertise. I'll provide regular summaries, and you can intervene whenever necessary. You remain the decision-makers."

To maintain oversight, Arjun set up checkpoints. Every week, he reviewed Maya's performance and flagged any anomalies. This system kept the balance between automation and control.

One unexpected benefit of automation was its positive impact on team morale.

Priya agreed. "It's like Maya's become the perfect assistant, always there to handle the grunt work, so we can shine."

As the ADAS project progressed, Maya's automation capabilities extended to other areas:

- **Budget Tracking**: Maya monitored expenses in real-time, flagging potential overruns.
- **Resource Management**: She tracked hardware inventory, ensuring components were available when needed.
- **Client Communications**: Maya drafted routine updates, freeing Arjun to focus on high-level discussions.

As Arjun sat with Priya and Ravi, their workday slowly winding down. The atmosphere was one of quiet reflection, with the trio mulling over the transformative journey they had undertaken with Maya by their side.

"Automation has transformed the way we work," Arjun began, his voice thoughtful yet tinged with excitement. "It's not just about cutting down repetitive tasks or streamlining processes. It's a paradigm shift. Maya isn't just a tool; she's become an extension of our team, a partner who helps us see the bigger picture."

Priya leaned forward, her eyes lighting up. "True, but I wonder, what's next? If Maya's capabilities have brought us this far, how do we leverage her potential to not just improve efficiency but redefine how we approach innovation itself?"

Ravi concurred, "A future where we focus purely on innovation while Maya handles the rest? Sign me up. But it's not just about automation, is it? It's about intelligence, adaptability, and scaling these capabilities across multiple projects. Imagine the ripple effect - one AI, many projects, and limitless possibilities."

Arjun nodded, his mind racing with ideas. "Think about it. Maya has already proven she can handle the complexities of an autonomous driving initiative. But what if we brought her into other domains? Healthcare, urban planning, even education projects that require a similar blend of precision and creativity. We could design a system where Maya doesn't just manage risks or optimize schedules; she could become the nexus of interconnected solutions, offering real-time insights that drive better outcomes across industries."

Priya chimed in, her voice tinged with wonder. "It's not just scaling Maya; it's creating a vision where humans and AI collaborate seamlessly. Imagine if every project team could have their version of Maya a personalized, intuitive AI that evolves with them, learning their quirks, adapting to their challenges, and driving them toward success."

Arjun leaned back, his eyes on the skyline outside. "But this vision also comes with responsibility. Scaling Maya means ensuring she remains transparent, ethical, and grounded in human values. Automation without empathy can't truly transform the world. Our job is to ensure that as we scale Maya, we also scale trust and accountability."

Priya smiled. "So, what's the next step? Do we build a framework for scaling Maya or focus on deepening her capabilities first?"

Arjun's eyes gleamed with determination. "Both. Let's create a roadmap that allows Maya to expand without losing her essence. And let's ensure that in every project she touches, she leaves behind not just success, but a legacy of how humans and AI can achieve the extraordinary together."

As the trio sat in silence, the weight of their shared vision settled in. It wasn't just about Maya anymore, it was about redefining the future of work, one project at a time.

Summary

This chapter explored how Maya's automation capabilities empowered the ADAS team to reclaim their time and focus on high-value tasks. By automating repetitive activities like reporting, task allocation, and resource tracking, the team achieved greater efficiency without losing control.

TASK

- **T**arget Routine Tasks: Identify areas where automation can save time.
- **A**ssess and Refine: Continuously improve automated workflows.
- **S**et Checkpoints: Maintain oversight to ensure quality and control.
- **K**eep Innovating: Use the time saved to focus on creative and strategic work.

Call to Action

Embrace automation as your taskmaster. Delegate the repetitive, focus on the impactful, and transform your productivity. Remember, automation isn't about replacement it's about empowerment

Step by Step Guide for Automation as Your Silent Partner

Imagine a world where you don't chase status updates, where dashboards build themselves, and where risks are flagged before they become bottlenecks. That world is already here, automation is your silent partner, ready to shoulder the weight of repetitive tasks, freeing your team to innovate.

Step 1: Identify Project Tasks to Automate

Think about the areas in your projects where time and energy are lost:

- **Status Reporting:** Automate weekly progress reports using tools like Power BI or Smartsheet that pull live data.
- **Risk Monitoring:** Deploy predictive analytics tools to track risks in real time. For instance, set up alerts for delayed dependencies or resource overutilization.
- **Stakeholder Communication:** Automate updates with tools like Monday.com to send dashboards directly to stakeholders.

Example:

In a software development project, tracking defects manually, delayed issue resolution. By integrating Jira with automated bug tracking alerts, the team reduced response times by 40%.

Step 2: Choose the Right Automation Tools

Automation thrives when paired with the right technology. Start by assessing your project's needs:

- **Dynamic Task Management:** Tools like ClickUp or Wrike can reassign tasks based on real-time changes in workload.
- **AI-Powered Resource Allocation:** Use AI systems like Runn or Float to optimize resource assignments dynamically.

- **Real-Time Collaboration:** Automate communication flows with tools like Slack bots or Microsoft Teams' Power Automate.

Example:

For a global ADAS project, time zone differences often delayed decision-making. A Slack bot was implemented to summarize key discussion points and notify decision-makers, ensuring nothing stalled overnight.

Step 3: Automate Workflow Pipelines

Map out your workflow and ask: What steps are manual, redundant, or error-prone?

- **Dependency Tracking:** Automate task linkages so that if one milestone slips, the entire schedule recalibrates.
- **Change Requests:** Use AI to analyze the impact of change requests instantly and suggest adjustments to timelines or budgets.
- **Testing & QA:** Set up automated test scripts for routine testing phases, freeing your QA team for exploratory testing.

Example:

During a hardware project, supplier delays were often flagged late. By automating supply chain monitoring, the team received early warnings when shipping patterns deviated, enabling proactive adjustments to assembly timelines.

Step 4: Implement Incrementally, Scale Holistically

- **Start small:** pilot one automation in a non-critical project phase and evaluate the results. Then expand to other areas once you've fine-tuned the process.
- **Pilot Example:** Automate time-tracking for team members using Toggl. Use the data to better estimate future project phases.

- **Scaling Example:** Extend this to automate cost forecasting based on time-tracking data, integrating with budgeting tools like Oracle Primavera.

Step 5: Build a Culture of Automation Trust

Automation succeeds when teams embrace it. Communicate its purpose clearly: it's a tool to empower them, not replace them. Train your teams to interpret automation outputs and combine them with their expertise.

Example:

During an IoT deployment project, Maya suggested reallocating tasks to balance workloads. Initially skeptical, team leads were trained on how Maya's predictions worked. Within weeks, the team reported higher satisfaction and on-time delivery improvements.

Your First Automation Mission

Take the leap today. Here's how:

1. **Choose One Workflow:** Identify the most time-consuming manual process in your project lifecycle.
   - Example: Task assignment during sprint planning. Automate this using Agile tools like Atlassian's Automation for Jira.
2. **Set Up Real-Time Alerts:** Enable AI-driven alerts for risks or bottlenecks, so you're always ahead of the curve.
   - Example: Use Trello or Azure to notify you when tasks exceed estimated durations.
3. **Review Impact Monthly:** Gather metrics on time saved, errors reduced, or efficiency gained. Use these insights to scale automation further.

Table: Project Management Tasks That Can Be Automated

Task Category	Specific Task	How to Automate	Tools/Technologies	Benefits
Planning	Project Scheduling	Use AI to generate project schedules based on input requirements, constraints, and resource availability.	Microsoft Project, Primavera, Smartsheet with AI modules	Reduces manual effort, ensures optimized timelines.
	Resource Allocation	Automate assignment of resources based on skills, availability, and workload.	Runn, Float, SAP AI	Ensures balanced workloads and prevents resource conflicts.
	Risk Identification	AI systems to scan historical data and current conditions to flag potential risks.	RiskLens, Planview, Jira	Predicts risks early, enabling proactive management.
	Cost Estim-ation	Generate cost breakdowns using historical data, scope inputs, and AI-based forecasts.	Oracle Primavera, Deltek Cobra	Provides more accurate cost predictions.
Execution	Task Management	Automatically assign and track tasks as project phases progress.	Asana, ClickUp, Monday.com	Saves time and ensures accountability.
	Change Request Management	Automate impact analysis for requested changes and notify stakeholders of updated timelines or budgets.	ServiceNow, Jira, Smartsheet	Streamlines decision-making for change requests.

Monito-ring	Status Repor-ting	Automate creation of weekly/ monthly status reports based on live project data.	Power BI, Tableau, Jira Automations	Frees up time spent on manual report preparation.
	KPI Tracking	Set up dashboards to monitor project KPIs such as progress, budget adherence, and resource utilization.	Power BI, Microsoft Teams	Real-time visibility into project health.
	Risk Monito-ring	Enable real-time risk tracking with automated alerts for new or evolving risks.	Riskwatch, RiskRadar	Helps address risks before they escalate.
	Communi-cation Updates	Automate stakeholder notifications based on project events or milestones.	Slack bots, Microsoft Teams workflows	Keeps stakeholders informed without manual effort.
Collabo-ration	Document Sharing	Automatically distribute updated documents to relevant team members or stakeholders.	Google Drive Automations, Dropbox Business	Ensures everyone has the latest information.
	Feedback Collection	Automate feedback surveys post-meeting or phase completion.	Typeform, SurveyMonkey, Microsoft Forms	Ensures timely and structured feedback.
Risk Manage-ment	Issue Escalation	Automatically escalate unresolved issues based on predefined thresholds.	Jira, ServiceNow	Ensures timely resolution of critical issues.
	Contin-gency Planning	AI-generated contingency plans for identified risks.	Palisade @RISK, Riskwatch	Prepares teams for potential disruptions.

Quality Assura-nce	Test Schedu-ling	Automate testing schedules and resource allocations based on project progress.	TestRail, Selenium Automations	Streamlines QA workflows.
	Error Track-ing	Automate detection and flagging of system errors or defects during testing phases.	Bugzilla, Jira with AI Plugins	Improves bug resolution speed.
Resource Manage-ment	Workload Balancing	Automate workload redistribution to avoid bottlenecks and burnout.	Float, Runn	Improves team efficiency and morale.
Budge-ting	Expense Tracking	Automate budget tracking and generate real-time alerts for deviations.	SAP Concur, QuickBooks	Prevents budget overruns.
	Invoice Manage-ment	Automate processing and approvals of vendor invoices.	Zoho Invoice, FreshBooks	Reduces delays in payments and errors.
Closing	Lessons Learned Documen-tation	Use AI to summarize project learnings from logs and communications.	Otter.ai, Notion	Saves effort in documenting project retrospectives.
	Post-Project Reviews	Automate creation of review reports, including success metrics and improvement areas.	Smartsheet, Google Sheets with Scripts	Provides structured and timely closure reports.
	Feedback Surveys	Schedule automated feedback forms for stakeholders after project completion.	SurveyMonkey, Microsoft Forms	Gathers insights for future projects.

Creative Additions

- **Innovation Opportunity Tracking**: AI can analyze project trends and flag opportunities for innovation or process improvements.
- **Team Sentiment Analysis**: Use AI to monitor team morale through email/communication tone and suggest interventions if morale dips.
- **Training Needs Detection**: AI flags gaps in team performance and suggests training modules based on individual performance data.

"When AI takes over the routine, you gain the freedom to focus on what truly matters."

— Ajay Tiwari

***

Chapter 9

The Connector: Building Bridges with Stakeholders

"Communication is the bridge between confusion and clarity."

— Nat Turner

Arjun was in the middle of reviewing a design flowchart when his phone buzzed. It was an unexpected call from a senior stakeholder, Mr. Rao, a critical investor in the ADAS project.

"Arjun, I've been hearing about delays in the project timeline. What's going on?"

The question sent a ripple of unease through Arjun. Delays? The project was slightly behind on one deliverable, but it was being resolved. Yet, perception mattered as much as reality when it came to stakeholder relationships.

"Mr. Rao, let me get you a detailed update right away," Arjun replied calmly, masking his internal panic. He turned to Maya.

"Maya, I need a status update tailored for Mr. Rao's concerns—detailed but concise, focused on deliverables and timelines. Can you help?"

Maya's screen lit up with reassuring confidence. "Of course, Arjun. Give me two minutes."

Within moments, Maya produced a summary designed specifically for Mr. Rao. It highlighted the project's progress, the minor delay, and the mitigation steps underway. Arjun forwarded it immediately, following up with a call to explain the situation personally.

"Thank you for this, Arjun. The transparency is reassuring," Mr. Rao said after hearing the update.

This incident highlighted a crucial truth: stakeholder management wasn't just about delivering results but also about maintaining trust through clear, proactive communication.

"Maya," Arjun said after the call, "can you help us communicate better with all stakeholders, not just in crisis moments?"

"Absolutely," Maya replied. "Let's build bridges, one message at a time."

Arjun and Maya began a new initiative: tailoring updates for different stakeholders.

Maya's ability to analyze individual preferences became invaluable. For instance:

- **Investors** like Mr. Rao valued financial insights and timeline projections.
- **Technical Partners** focused on progress in system development and technical hurdles.
- **End-Users** wanted to hear about real-world applications and benefits.

Using AI, Maya categorized stakeholders and created personalized dashboards for each group.

"Instead of sending generic updates, we'll give everyone the information they care about most," Maya explained.

Arjun noticed immediate results. Stakeholders appreciated the relevance of the updates, leading to fewer questions and more trust in the team's direction.

One day, Maya alerted Arjun to a subtle but concerning trend.

"Sentiment analysis suggests dissatisfaction among a subset of stakeholders. Their feedback on recent updates is becoming more negative."

Maya had been analyzing email replies, meeting transcripts, and even stakeholder survey results. By detecting patterns in tone and language, she flagged potential issues early.

"Let's address this head-on," Arjun decided.

He scheduled one-on-one calls with the concerned stakeholders, using Maya's insights to prepare. By anticipating their concerns, he could respond effectively, turning potential dissatisfaction into a constructive dialogue.

Arjun realized that stakeholders valued not just good news but honest, transparent communication.

During a project review meeting, Maya presented a risk report detailing potential supply chain delays. Instead of glossing over the issue, Arjun addressed it directly.

"We're aware of the challenge, and here's how we're mitigating it," he explained, showcasing Maya's predictive models and contingency plans.

Stakeholders appreciated the openness. Priya later commented, "The transparency isn't just about keeping them informed—it's about making them part of the solution."

Maya also helped Arjun strengthen relationships by proactively identifying opportunities to engage stakeholders.

"Arjun," Maya suggested one morning, "Mr. Singh, one of the government regulators, has shown interest in the project's safety testing results. Perhaps sharing more details could build goodwill."

Arjun acted on the suggestion, inviting Mr. Singh to visit the testing facility. The gesture was well-received, further solidifying the project's credibility.

The ADAS project involved a diverse network of stakeholders, from technical experts and investors to regulatory bodies and end-users. Managing their varying expectations was a delicate balancing act.

Maya became a central hub for communication. She tracked stakeholder interactions, ensuring follow-ups weren't missed and messages remained consistent.

During a stakeholder alignment meeting, Maya displayed an interactive map of all stakeholders, their roles, and their priorities.

"This is incredible," Priya said, examining the map. "It's like having a bird's-eye view of the entire network."

One of the most challenging moments came when a rumor circulated about the ADAS project's safety features being subpar.

Maya immediately flagged the issue through sentiment analysis on social media and internal communications.

"Arjun, we need to act quickly," Maya warned. "The sentiment trend could escalate if left unaddressed."

Arjun and the team crafted a response strategy with Maya's help. They hosted a webinar showcasing the rigorous testing processes, using AI-generated simulations to demonstrate safety features.

The crisis was averted, and stakeholders praised the team's proactive approach.

Despite Maya's impressive capabilities, Arjun was careful not to let technology replace genuine human interaction.

During quarterly review meetings, he made it a point to engage stakeholders personally. Maya prepared detailed talking points, but Arjun added his own insights and anecdotes.

"Maya makes our communication precise," he explained to Priya, "but trust is built through human connection."

As the project neared its next milestone, Arjun began exploring how Maya's communication capabilities could scale.

"Maya," he asked one evening, "can we automate stakeholder updates while keeping them personalized?"

Maya's response was immediate. "We can create an automated update system with customizable templates for each stakeholder group. It will save time while maintaining relevance."

The system was a success. Weekly updates went out seamlessly, keeping everyone informed without adding to the team's workload.

Reflecting on the journey, Arjun saw how far the team had come. Maya had transformed stakeholder communication from a reactive effort into a proactive strategy.

"Maya isn't just a tool," Arjun told Priya and Krishna during a team meeting. "She's become our bridge-builder, connecting us with every stakeholder in meaningful ways."

Priya smiled. "It's amazing how AI can enhance relationships without replacing the human touch."

Summary

This chapter demonstrated how Maya's AI-driven insights transformed stakeholder communication. By tailoring updates, analyzing sentiments, and providing actionable predictions, Maya helped the team build trust and strengthen relationships.

BRIDGE

- **B**uild Transparency: Share honest updates, even when delivering bad news.
- **R**espond Proactively: Use AI insights to address concerns before they escalate.
- **I**dentify Priorities: Customize communication based on stakeholder needs.
- **D**evelop Relationships: Engage stakeholders with meaningful interactions.
- **G**row Engagement: Use AI to scale and personalize updates.
- **E**mpower Connection: Balance AI automation with a human touch.

Call to Action

Leverage AI as your connector. Build bridges with stakeholders through transparency, tailored communication, and proactive engagement. Remember, strong relationships are the foundation of every successful project!

Leveraging AI to Build Stakeholder Bridges

To implement the principles from Chapter 9 effectively, project managers can focus on integrating AI into relationship management with stakeholders. Below is a detailed **action plan with examples** and an accompanying table listing specific PM tasks for automation related to stakeholder engagement.

Action Plan with Examples

1. **Enhance Stakeholder Communication**
   - **Example**: Use AI-powered sentiment analysis on stakeholder emails to understand their concerns better and adjust your tone accordingly.

- **How**: Set up tools like Grammarly Insights or Crystal Knows for tone adjustment and emotional cues.

2. **Provide Real-Time Updates**
   - **Example**: Deploy automated dashboards tailored for each stakeholder group. A client-facing dashboard could show delivery progress, while internal dashboards focus on resource utilization.
   - **How**: Use platforms like Power BI or Tableau to customize and automate updates.
3. **Anticipate Stakeholder Needs**
   - **Example**: Maya detects recurring delays during approval processes and recommends notifying specific stakeholders in advance to speed up reviews.
   - **How**: Integrate AI tools that analyze historical data, such as Jira's AI-driven workflows.
4. **Personalize Engagement**
   - **Example**: Tailor communication frequency based on stakeholder preferences. Maya could send weekly summaries to high-involvement stakeholders and monthly overviews to low-engagement ones.
   - **How**: Use AI-driven CRM tools like Salesforce Einstein to automate tailored communication.
5. **Proactively Solve Issues**
   - **Example**: During a project, AI identifies a potential misalignment between client expectations and actual deliverables. Proactively schedule a clarification call.
   - **How**: Use AI assistants like Clara or x.ai for scheduling and coordination.

Table: Stakeholder Management Tasks That Can Be Automated

Task Category	Specific Task	How to Automate	Tools/ Technologies	Benefits
Communi-cation	Automated Status Updates	Set up auto-generated updates tailored for different stakeholder groups.	Power BI, Tableau, Zoho Projects	Reduces manual reporting efforts and keeps stakeholders informed.
	Sentiment Analysis	Analyze stakeholder feedback (emails, meetings) to gauge sentiment and concerns.	Grammarly Insights, Crystal Knows	Helps identify and address dissatis-faction early.
	Meeting Summaries	Automatically summarize key decisions and action points post-meetings.	Otter.ai, Fireflies.ai	Saves time in documenting discussions and ensures clarity.
	Tailored Communi-cation	Automate delivery of customized emails or reports based on stakeholder preferences.	Salesforce Einstein, HubSpot CRM	Builds trust through personali-zation.
Engage-ment	Scheduling Stakeholder Meetings	AI tools to schedule and coordinate meetings across multiple time zones.	Clara, x.ai	Simplifies scheduling and ensures alignment.

	Proactive Issue Notifications	Identify potential risks/issues and notify stakeholders with context and proposed solutions.	Jira, Slack Integrations	Prevents escalation by keeping stakeholders in the loop early.
Risk Manage-ment	Stakeholder Impact Analysis	Use AI to analyze how changes impact different stakeholder groups.	Planview, RiskLens	Enhances decision-making with stake-holder conside-rations.
	Approval Workflow Automation	Automate and prioritize approval requests based on urgency and stakeholder hierarchy.	Kissflow, Pipefy	Reduces bottlenecks in approval processes.
Feedback Collection	Post-Milestone Feedback Surveys	Automate collection and analysis of stakeholder feedback after key project milestones.	SurveyMonkey, Microsoft Forms	Provides structured feedback for continuous improve-ment.
	Stakeholder Sentiment Tracking	Continuously monitor stakeholder sentiments during the project lifecycle.	IBM Watson Tone Analyzer, Slack Bots	Helps refine communi-cation and engagement strategies.
Reporting	Stakeholder-Specific Dashboards	Generate dashboards that cater to the specific interests of different stakeholder groups.	Tableau, Power BI	Improves transparency and builds trust.

Align-ment	Expectations vs. Deliverables Tracking	AI compares stakeholder expectations with project deliverables in real time.	Trello with Butler, Notion Automations	Ensures alignment and minimizes misunder-standings.
Collabo-ration	Shared Document Management	Automate sharing of updated documents with relevant stakeholders.	Google Workspace, Dropbox	Ensures everyone is always working with the latest information.
	Decision Logs	Automatically log key decisions and their justifications for transparency.	Confluence, Evernote Automations	Keeps a clear record of all stakeholder discussions.

"AI becomes the bridge that connects you to your stakeholders, fostering trust, transparency, and collaboration."

— Ajay Tiwari

***

Chapter 10

Guardrails and Grey Areas: AI's Limits and Ethics

"Technology is a tool, but ethics are a compass."

— Ajay Tiwari

The ADAS project was progressing smoothly—or so Arjun thought. One morning, Maya's voice broke through the usual buzz of the office.

"Arjun, I need your attention. There's an anomaly in the supplier evaluation metrics."

Arjun frowned. "What kind of anomaly?"

Maya displayed a chart on the screen. A key supplier's rating had dropped significantly due to an algorithm flagging inconsistencies in their historical data. The issue wasn't apparent during manual reviews.

"We need to dig deeper," Arjun said, looping Priya into the conversation.

As they analyzed the data, Priya asked, "How sure are we that Maya isn't overestimating the problem? Could this be a false flag?"

The question lingered, marking the beginning of a journey to understand AI's limitations—and the ethical dilemmas tied to its use.

Later that day, Arjun convened a team meeting. "Maya has been a game-changer, but today's situation reminds me of something important. We must remember that AI, while powerful, isn't infallible."

Priya nodded. "Maya's outputs are only as good as the data and algorithms behind them. If the data has bias or gaps, the recommendations could be flawed."

The team discussed examples:

- A hiring AI that favored certain demographics due to biased training data.
- Financial models that penalized smaller vendors based on outdated assumptions.

Ravi added, "It's tempting to treat AI like an oracle, but we have to stay vigilant. It's a tool, not a replacement for critical thinking."

The team was finalizing the allocation of resources for the next project phase. Maya recommended prioritizing a specific supplier for a critical component based on cost-efficiency. However, Arjun noticed a potential issue: the supplier had questionable labor practices.

"Maya," Arjun asked, "did the algorithm account for ethical considerations when making this recommendation?"

"No," Maya replied. "The evaluation focused on cost, reliability, and timeliness."

Arjun sighed. "This is a grey area. Do we go with the supplier for efficiency or choose another option that aligns with our values?"

The team debated the decision. In the end, they decided to prioritize ethical sourcing, even if it meant higher costs.

"This isn't just about numbers," Arjun said. "It's about who we are as a team and the standards we set."

Priya proposed a new initiative: improving transparency in how Maya's algorithms made decisions.

"We need to understand the 'why' behind Maya's recommendations," she said.

Krishna worked with Maya to implement explainable AI (XAI) modules. These modules allowed the team to view the factors influencing Maya's outputs.

"It's like pulling back the curtain," Krishna explained during a demonstration. "We can now see the weightage given to each parameter - cost, timeline, risk, and so on."

This transparency boosted confidence in Maya's recommendations and highlighted areas where human judgment was needed.

One afternoon, Maya flagged an issue in a dataset used for risk predictions.

"Arjun, I've identified potential bias in the historical project data," Maya announced. "Smaller vendors are disproportionately flagged as high-risk."

Arjun reviewed the dataset and realized it was skewed. Past projects had favored larger vendors, leading to biased risk evaluations.

"We need to correct this," he said.

Priya and Krishna collaborated to cleanse the dataset, ensuring future analyses were fairer. The team also introduced a periodic review process to identify and address biases proactively.

As Maya became integral to the project, Arjun noticed a subtle shift in the team's dynamics.

"I think we're leaning on Maya a bit too much," he confided to Priya one evening.

Priya agreed. "Maya's great for handling complexity, but we can't let it replace our instincts and experience."

To recalibrate, Arjun introduced a simple rule: **Every AI recommendation must be reviewed by a human.**

"AI isn't here to replace us," he reminded the team. "It's here to make us better."

The team began exploring hypothetical scenarios to sharpen their understanding of AI ethics.

- **Scenario 1:** An AI model predicts that a particular feature will fail in 10% of use cases. Should the team proceed with the feature, delay the project to fix it, or remove it altogether?

- **Scenario 2:** A competitor offers an AI-powered tool with questionable data privacy practices. Should they adopt it to stay competitive or prioritize ethical concerns?

Each scenario sparked lively debates, reinforcing the importance of ethical considerations in decision-making.

Over time, the team developed a set of "guardrails" to guide their use of AI:

1. **Data Integrity:** Regularly review and cleanse datasets to minimize bias.
2. **Explain ability:** Ensure AI decisions are transparent and understandable.
3. **Human Oversight:** Require human approval for critical AI-driven decisions.

4. **Ethical Standards:** Align AI usage with the team's values and principles.
5. **Continuous Learning:** Stay informed about AI advancements and potential pitfalls.

Reflecting on their journey, Arjun addressed the team.

"Maya has shown us what's possible, but today's lessons remind us to proceed with caution. AI is only as good as the people guiding it."

Maya chimed in. **"And I'm here to learn and grow with you."**

The room filled with laughter, but the message was clear: the future of AI in project management depended on balancing its strengths with human wisdom and ethical responsibility.

Summary

This chapter explored the ethical and practical limitations of AI, illustrating how Maya's capabilities required human oversight and integrity. From addressing data bias to navigating ethical dilemmas, the team learned to approach AI with caution and respect.

ETHICS

- **E**valuate Bias: Regularly review datasets for fairness.
- **T**ransparency: Make AI decisions explainable.
- **H**uman Oversight: Pair AI with critical thinking.
- **I**ntegrity: Align AI use with core values.
- **C**ollaborate: Use AI as a partner, not a replacement.
- **S**ustain Learning: Continuously adapt and improve.

Call to Action

As you integrate AI into your projects, remember its potential and limitations. Approach every decision with ETHICS - balancing the power of AI with the responsibility of human judgment. Only then can we harness technology for the greater good!

Ethics in Action: Become the Leader AI Needs

As you embark on your AI journey, embrace the role of a responsible innovator. Make decisions that combine the analytical precision of AI with the wisdom of human ethics. Here's how to start today:

- **Challenge the Status Quo:** Question every recommendation and decision with a lens of fairness and transparency.
- **Adopt the ETHICS Framework:** Use Evaluate, Transparency, Human Oversight, Integrity, Collaboration, and Sustain Learning as your compass.
- **Be the Voice of Accountability:** In every project, lead discussions on AI's limitations and biases. Inspire your team to hold AI to the same high standards as themselves.
- **Turn Grey Areas into Guiding Lights:** Use challenges as opportunities to reinforce your team's values. Commit to decisions that prioritize integrity over convenience.

Every project is a chance to redefine the relationship between AI and humanity. Take that step—responsibly, creatively, and ethically.

Table of Ethical Scenarios and Guardrails

This table aligns with the ethical challenges and guidelines for AI usage in project management.

Ethical Scenario	Key Challenge	Proposed Guardrail
Bias in Supplier Evaluation Metrics	Data skew favors larger vendors.	Regular audits and cleansing of datasets to minimize inherent bias.
Overemphasis on Cost-Efficiency in Recommendations	Ignores ethical labor practices.	Introduce parameters for ethical considerations into evaluation criteria.
Over-Reliance on AI Outputs for Critical Decisions	Risk of sidelining human judgment.	Mandate human review for all AI-driven decisions, especially those with ethical implications.

Opaque Decision-Making by AI	Lack of trust in AI recommendations.	Implement Explainable AI (XAI) to ensure transparency in decision-making processes.
AI-Driven Hiring Practices	Potential for demographic biases.	Evaluate AI models for fairness; include human oversight in the recruitment process.
Data Privacy Concerns with Third-Party AI Tools	Breach of trust or regulatory issues.	Ensure compliance with data protection laws and use AI tools vetted for privacy.
Unethical Competitor AI Practices	Temptation to compromise on values.	Establish a code of conduct for AI use and advocate for ethical AI standards in the industry.
Prioritization of AI Efficiency Over Stakeholder Values	Misalignment with organizational culture.	Engage stakeholders to co-create AI guidelines that reflect shared values.

Following action points to ponder for you,

1. **Scenario Challenges:** Create a reflective activity where readers assess an ethical scenario they've faced or anticipate. Ask: "How would you apply the ETHICS framework to solve this?"
2. **Toolkit Creation:** Encourage readers to draft their personalized "AI Ethics Toolkit" using their industry's challenges.
3. **Real-World Pledge:** Prompt readers to write a commitment statement to align AI usage with ethical standards in their projects.
4. **Collaborative Learning:** Recommend organizing team discussions to debate ethical dilemmas, fostering a culture of shared responsibility.

"AI is a powerful ally, but it's up to us to set the boundaries and ensure it serves humanity with fairness and integrity."

— Ajay Tiwari

***

Chapter 11

The Growth Mindset: Cultivating Your AI-Enhanced Skills

"The growth mindset doesn't just change what you do; it changes how you see the world."

— Carol Dweck

The ADAS project was in its final phase, and the office buzzed with anticipation. After months of grappling with challenges, leveraging Maya's capabilities, and navigating the ethical grey areas, Arjun reflected on how far the team had come.

One evening, as the Sun dipped below the horizon, Priya approached Arjun at his desk. "You look deep in thought," she said.

"I was just thinking about how this journey with Maya has reshaped us," Arjun replied. "It's not just about AI anymore. It's about how we've evolved alongside it."

Their conversation sparked an idea: a retrospective session with the team to distill the lessons they'd learned and prepare for what lay ahead.

The next day, the team gathered in the conference room. Maya, as always, was ready to assist.

Arjun began, "Today's session isn't about work. It's about growth—our growth as professionals and as a team."

The team revisited key moments from the project:

- **The Planning Oracle:** Using Maya to predict timelines and resource needs.
- **The Risk Shield:** Catching potential pitfalls before they became problems.
- **The Collaborator:** Streamlining teamwork and communication.
- **The Taskmaster:** Delegating repetitive tasks to reclaim time.
- **The Connector:** Building trust with stakeholders through tailored updates.
- **The Guardrails:** Navigating AI's limits and ethical challenges.

Krishna shared, "For me, the biggest takeaway was learning that AI isn't here to replace us it's here to enhance us. But only if we keep questioning and improving it."

During the retrospective, Priya pointed out an incident that hadn't involved Maya directly.

"Do you remember when the user feedback loop revealed an unexpected issue with the interface design?" she asked.

Arjun nodded. "Yes, Maya didn't flag it because it wasn't data-driven. It was a subtle usability issue that only became apparent through user testing."

The issue highlighted an important lesson: while AI could analyze patterns and predict outcomes, some problems required human intuition, empathy, and creativity.

"AI is powerful," Priya said, "but it can't replace the human ability to understand the nuances of user experience or cultural contexts."

Arjun posed a question to the team: "How do we ensure we keep growing alongside AI?"

The discussion led to several strategies:

1. **Stay Updated on AI Trends:**

   Priya shared resources like industry journals, online courses, and webinars. "We need to stay informed about advancements and emerging best practices," she said.

2. **Sharpen Critical Thinking:**

   "We can't afford to get complacent," Krishna added. "Even with Maya, we have to validate recommendations and challenge assumptions."

3. **Blend Soft and Hard Skills:**

   Arjun emphasized the importance of communication, empathy, and adaptability. "The best project managers of the future will be those who combine AI expertise with human-centric skills."

4. **Experiment and Iterate:**

   The team agreed on the value of experimentation. "Every project is an opportunity to try new things and learn," Priya said.

5. **Foster a Growth Mindset:**

   "Above all," Arjun concluded, "we must view AI not as a destination but as a journey. Each project, each challenge, is a step forward."

As the project neared completion, Arjun looked ahead to future challenges.

Maya, ever the supportive assistant, chimed in. **"Arjun, you've taught me as much as I've taught you. I look forward to our next adventure."**

The team laughed, but the sentiment resonated. Maya wasn't just a tool; she was a partner in their growth.

Months later, Arjun was invited to a conference on AI in project management. His keynote speech, titled "The Growth Mindset: Evolving with AI," drew on the team's journey.

He shared the story of the ADAS project, emphasizing the importance of staying curious, adaptable, and ethical.

"AI is a powerful ally," he told the audience. "But it's true potential is unlocked when we commit to growing alongside it - questioning, learning, and evolving every step of the way."

Summary

This chapter emphasized the importance of viewing AI as a journey rather than just a tool. Through the ADAS project, the team learned to balance AI's strengths with human intuition, addressing unseen challenges and fostering continuous growth. Key takeaways included staying updated on AI advancements, honing critical thinking, blending soft and hard skills, and maintaining a growth mindset.

GROWTH

- **G**ather Knowledge: Stay updated on AI trends and tools.
- **R**efine Skills: Blend technical expertise with empathy and creativity.
- **O**pen to Feedback: Learn from experiences and adapt strategies.
- **W**elcome Challenges: View each obstacle as a learning opportunity.
- **T**eam Collaboration: Leverage AI to enhance, not replace, teamwork.
- **H**uman Connection: Remember the value of intuition and empathy.

Call to Action

Your AI journey doesn't end here it begins now. Embrace the **GROWTH** mindset and commit to evolving with AI. Stay curious, stay ethical, and let every project be a step forward in your journey as a modern, AI-enhanced project manager!

Action Plan with Examples

1. **G – Gather Knowledge Continuously**
    - **Example**: Attend AI-focused webinars or courses like "AI in Project Management" on Coursera or LinkedIn Learning.
    - **How**: Allocate one hour weekly for professional development.

2. **R – Refine Ethical Practices**
    - **Example:** Establish a data privacy policy when using AI tools for stakeholder communication to ensure compliance with GDPR or similar regulations.
    - **How:** Use AI tools like TrustArc or OneTrust to automate privacy assessments.

3. **O – Optimize Processes**
   - **Example:** Use AI to reduce manual workload in resource allocation by analyzing team availability and skills.
   - **How:** Tools like ClickUp's AI or Resource Guru can suggest optimal resource distribution.
4. **W – Work Smarter, Not Harder**
   - **Example**: Deploy AI assistants like Trello's Butler or Notion AI to automate repetitive tasks such as updating task statuses or sending reminders.
   - **How**: Integrate these tools into your project management platforms.
5. **T – Transform Team Collaboration**
   - **Example**: Use AI tools for real-time language translation during global stakeholder meetings, ensuring inclusivity.
   - **How**: Use platforms like Microsoft Teams with Translator AI integration.
6. **H – Harness AI for Innovation**
   - **Example**: During ideation sessions, let AI like ChatGPT generate creative solutions or identify trends from data.
   - **How**: Incorporate AI during brainstorming or strategy planning meetings.

AI is your co-pilot, but you're still in the captain's seat. As you navigate through the evolving AI landscape, remember to:

- **Set Guardrails:** Regularly evaluate the ethics of your AI tools.
- **Question the Grey Areas:** Embrace uncertainty as an opportunity for growth and alignment with your values.
- **Foster Accountability:** Implement transparent systems to track and justify AI decisions.
- **Balance the Equation:** Pair AI's capabilities with your wisdom, ethics, and creativity.

- Let these principles guide your journey, making every decision a responsible and impactful one.

PM Tasks and Potential for Automation

Here's a table showcasing key project management tasks with a focus on automation potential while ensuring alignment with AI's limitations and ethical considerations:

PM Task	Can Be Automated? (Yes/ Partial/No)	Automation Details
Task Scheduling and Updates	Yes	AI can generate schedules, update timelines, and adjust based on dependencies.
Risk Identification	Partial	AI detects patterns and flags potential risks, but human judgment is needed for nuance.
Resource Allocation	Yes	AI optimizes resource assignments based on skills, availability, and timelines.
Stakeholder Communication	Partial	AI drafts updates, but PMs must review for tone, context, and relationship nuances.
Supplier Evaluation	Partial	AI analyzes performance metrics, but ethical considerations must be human-driven.
Budget Tracking	Yes	Automates expense tracking and alerts for deviations, requiring oversight for adjustments.
Quality Assurance	Partial	AI flags defects or deviations in data but relies on human inspection for user-experience nuances.
Data Analysis and Reporting	Yes	AI creates dashboards and insights from large datasets quickly and accurately.
Decision Support	Partial	AI provides recommendations, but final decisions depend on ethical and strategic inputs.
Team Collaboration Tools Management	Yes	AI streamlines task delegation, meeting scheduling, and knowledge sharing.

Ethics Compliance Review	No	Human-driven to evaluate alignment with organizational and societal values.
Change Management	Partial	AI identifies impacted areas and suggests adjustments; execution needs human empathy.
Conflict Resolution	No	A purely human task requiring empathy, intuition, and relational skills.
Performance Metrics Tracking	Yes	AI aggregates data and tracks KPIs, providing alerts for trends or anomalies.
Feedback Collection and Analysis	Partial	AI collects and analyzes feedback; human interpretation is needed for actionable insights.

- **Guardrails for Automation:** Implement controls like data audits and explainable AI to ensure ethical decision-making.
- **Grey Areas in Automation:** Identify tasks where human oversight is crucial, like conflict resolution or supplier ethics.
- **Transparency Tools:** Use tools like Explainable AI (XAI) modules to clarify AI decision-making processes.

The AI-Enhanced PM Mantra

GROWTH isn't just a mindset it's a strategy. Embrace automation where it adds value, collaborate with AI like a team member, and let every project become a testament to your evolution as a project manager. **The future belongs to those who build it, one AI-powered decision at a time.**

"Embrace AI not as a destination, but as a journey that will continuously evolve your skills and expand your possibilities."

— Ajay Tiwari

***

Conclusion: The Next Frontier

"The future is not something we enter. The future is something we create."

— Leonard I. Sweet

As Arjun stepped into the final presentation for the ADAS project, he couldn't help but feel a sense of accomplishment. The journey with Maya and the team had been transformative, not only for the project's success but also for their personal growth as professionals in the AI era.

The ADAS system was ready to make its debut, and every stakeholder was eager to see the results. What began as a daunting challenge had become a masterclass in AI-enhanced project management. From planning and risk mitigation to automation and stakeholder communication, the team had harnessed Maya's capabilities to push boundaries.

The room filled with applause as Arjun concluded the presentation. But even as the project wrapped up, he knew this wasn't the end of the story - it was just the beginning.

Later that evening, Arjun sat with Priya and Krishna in the office lounge, sharing a celebratory cup of coffee.

"You know," Priya said, "when we started this project, I thought AI was just a tool. But Maya has been so much more than that she's been an invisible ally every step of the way."

Krishna nodded. "True. But what's fascinating is how you all 've grown with Maya. She's taught as much as you all 've taught her. It's a symbiotic relationship."

Arjun smiled. "That's the essence of AI in project management. It's not about replacing us; it's about elevating us. Maya was never here to make decisions for us - she was here to make us better decision-makers."

The team recounted their favorite moments from the project, from the initial planning phases to the unforeseen challenges Maya had helped them navigate. But they also reflected on moments where human intuition and creativity had filled the gaps Maya couldn't address.

The conversation shifted to the future.

"Where do we go from here?" Priya asked.

"The next frontier," Arjun replied. "This project has shown us the power of AI at a foundational level. But there's so much more to explore - intermediate and advanced applications that can revolutionize how we manage projects."

Arjun explained his vision for the future of AI in project management:

- **Dynamic Adaptability:** Leveraging AI to not only predict changes but to adapt project plans in real time.
- **Cross-Disciplinary Integration:** Using AI to bridge gaps between departments, ensuring seamless collaboration across diverse teams.
- **Ethical Innovation:** Pushing the boundaries of AI while staying grounded in ethical principles and transparency.
- **Predictive Insights at Scale:** Scaling AI's predictive capabilities to manage mega-projects with multiple interdependent components.
- **Enhanced Personalization:** Creating AI systems that learn and adapt to the unique styles and preferences of each project manager.

"We've scratched the surface," Arjun said. "The next steps will involve diving deeper into these areas, mastering not just AI's capabilities but also our own roles in shaping its potential."

As if on cue, Maya's interface lit up on the large screen in the lounge.

"Arjun and Priya," Maya began, her tone imbued with a warmth that felt almost human. "It's been an honor to assist you on this journey. But remember, I am only as effective as the humans who guide me. You've shown me what true collaboration looks like."

Maya's words struck a chord. She wasn't just a piece of software; she was a reflection of their collective growth.

"Thank you, Maya," Arjun said. "We couldn't have done it without you."

"Nor I without you," Maya replied. "Here's to the next frontier."

Before leaving for the day, Arjun shared a sneak peek of his plans with Priya and Krishna.

"I'm working on a framework for intermediate and advanced AI applications in project management," he revealed. "It'll cover topics like real-time adaptive systems, ethical AI governance, and multi-project optimization."

Priya's eyes lit up. "That sounds incredible. Count me in!"

Krishna added, "If this project was the foundation, I can't wait to see what we build next."

Walking out of the office that night, Arjun paused to take in the view of the city skyline. The ADAS project had been a milestone, but it was also a reminder of the limitless potential AI offered.

He thought about the lessons Maya had taught them: the importance of balance, the value of intuition, and the power of continuous learning. AI wasn't just a tool—it was a catalyst for personal and professional transformation.

Summary

The conclusion chapter encapsulates the team's journey with Maya, emphasizing AI as an invisible ally that complements human intuition and creativity. It highlights the transformation AI brings to project management while setting the stage for more advanced applications in the future. Key lessons include viewing AI as a partner, embracing continuous growth, and balancing AI's capabilities with ethical considerations.

FRONTIER

Your relationship with AI is not static - it's dynamic, evolving with every challenge and insight. Adopt the **FRONTIER** mindset to push boundaries while remaining ethically grounded. Here are actionable steps to explore your next AI frontiers:

1. **Frame Your Vision:** Start with a clear goal for integrating AI into your project. Define how it can enhance efficiency and decision-making.
2. **Reevaluate Constantly:** Periodically assess AI's impact on your project. Is it solving the right problems or creating new challenges?
3. **Open Collaboration:** Foster a culture of transparency and ethical AI discussions within your team.
4. **Navigate Ethical Dilemmas:** Use the **FRONTIER** framework as a compass to balance progress with responsibility.
5. **Train for Tomorrow:** Upskill in AI technologies and ethical considerations. Keep your knowledge as dynamic as the tools you use.
6. **Innovate Boldly:** Pilot experimental AI approaches on non-critical project areas to learn from outcomes.
7. **Evaluate Results:** Measure AI's effectiveness beyond numbers—consider stakeholder trust, ethical practices, and long-term value.
8. **Reimagine What's Next:** Let every success and setback inspire you to redefine AI's role in your professional journey.

Call to Action

Your journey with AI doesn't end here - it's just the beginning. Embrace the **FRONTIER** mindset and prepare to explore the next level of AI-enhanced project management. Stay curious, stay ethical, and let every step take you closer to mastering this transformative technology. The next frontier awaits!

The frontier is vast, but with vision, vigilance, and a focus on ethical progress, it becomes your playground for innovation.

Table: Applying the FRONTIER Mindset to AI-Enhanced Project Management

FRONTIER Element	Actionable Steps	Project Examples
F – Frame Your Vision	Define a specific objective for AI integration.	Use AI to streamline risk management by identifying bottlenecks in the project pipeline.
R – Reevaluate Constantly	Conduct periodic reviews of AI's performance.	Assess if AI-driven supplier evaluations remain fair and accurate as new data comes in.
O – Open Collaboration	Create spaces for discussing AI's impact and ethics within the team.	Host weekly sessions to explore ethical dilemmas posed by AI recommendations (e.g., balancing cost-efficiency with labor ethics).
N – Navigate Ethical Dilemmas	Establish guidelines for ethical decision-making with AI.	Develop rules such as "No critical decision relies on AI without human oversight."
T – Train for Tomorrow	Invest in team learning about AI trends and ethical practices.	Provide access to AI workshops and courses focused on explainable AI (XAI) and data bias mitigation.
I – Innovate Boldly	Experiment with AI in non-critical areas to test new capabilities.	Pilot AI-powered stakeholder sentiment analysis to predict and address communication challenges.
E – Evaluate Results	Look beyond metrics to assess AI's impact on trust and values.	Compare project results pre- and post-AI integration, focusing on quality, inclusivity, and alignment with stakeholder expectations.
R – Reimagine What's Next	Apply lessons from each project to expand AI's role in future initiatives.	Plan the next project phase to include AI-driven task prioritization with built-in ethical checks.

Examples of Creative Activities for Call to Action

1. **Team Charter on AI:** Ask project teams to draft a one-page charter outlining their principles for ethical AI usage in upcoming projects.
2. **Personal Reflection Prompt:** Encourage readers to write about one ethical challenge they foresee with AI in their industry and how they'd address it using the FRONTIER mindset.
3. **Case Study Creation:** Provide a template for documenting AI use cases in their projects, noting successes, pitfalls, and lessons learned for future reference.
4. **Future-Proof Plan:** Motivate readers to create a three-month roadmap for exploring AI's next potential in their field, including specific tools, training, and pilot projects.

"The invisible ally is just the beginning. As you master AI, you unlock new horizons of potential, opportunity, and innovation."

— Ajay Tiwari

***

References

The following resources were consulted and recommended for further reading to deepen your understanding of AI, project management, and related topics.

Books

1. Russell, S., & Norvig, P. (2020). Artificial Intelligence: A Modern Approach (4th Edition). Pearson Education.
   - A comprehensive introduction to the field of artificial intelligence, covering fundamental concepts and practical applications.
2. Kerzner, H. (2022). Project Management: A Systems Approach to Planning, Scheduling, and Controlling (13th Edition). Wiley.
   - A classic guide to project management methodologies and tools.
3. Sharma, P. (2021). AI in Project Management: Adapting to the New Normal. Springer.
   - Explores the role of AI in enhancing traditional project management practices.

Research Papers and Articles

4. Brynjolfsson, E., & McAfee, A. (2017). The Business of Artificial Intelligence: What It Can — and Cannot — Do for Your Organization. Harvard Business Review.
   - Examines the practical implications of AI in business operations, including project management.
5. Davenport, T., & Ronanki, R. (2018). Artificial Intelligence for the Real World. Harvard Business Review.
   - A practical framework for identifying where AI can add value in organizational contexts.
6. Jung, Y., & Woo, J. (2020). A Study on Predictive Analytics Using AI in Project Risk Management. Journal of Project Management Research.
   - Discusses how predictive analytics powered by AI can identify and mitigate risks in projects.

Web Resources

7. PMI.org – Project Management Institute
   - Offers extensive resources on project management frameworks, trends, and certifications.
   - https://www.pmi.org
8. Towards Data Science – AI and Machine Learning in Business Applications
   - Regularly updated articles on AI technologies and their real-world applications.
   - https://towardsdatascience.com
9. Kaggle.com – Datasets and AI Solutions
   - A platform for AI practitioners to access data and collaborate on predictive solutions.
   - https://www.kaggle.com

Tools and Platforms

10. Asana, Trello, and Monday.com
    - Examples of AI-enabled project management tools that offer features like task automation and real-time tracking.
11. IBM Watson
    - AI-powered solutions for decision-making and process optimization in business.
    - https://www.ibm.com/watson
12. Microsoft Power BI
    - A tool for data visualization and AI-driven business analytics.
    - https://powerbi.microsoft.com

Case Studies and Industry Reports

13. McKinsey Global Institute (2021). The State of AI in 2021.
    - Provides an overview of AI adoption trends and success stories across industries.
    - https://www.mckinsey.com/mgi
14. Gartner (2022). Hype Cycle for Artificial Intelligence.
    - Explains the maturity and business value of various AI technologies.
    - https://www.gartner.com

These references provide a mix of foundational knowledge, real-world insights, and advanced strategies to complement your learning from this book.

Additional References

Books

15. Gartner, J. (2019). AI Superpowers: China, Silicon Valley, and the New World Order. Houghton Mifflin Harcourt.
    - A deep dive into the AI revolution and its impact on global industries.
16. Silver, N. (2015). The Signal and the Noise: Why So Many Predictions Fail – but Some Don't. Penguin Books.
    - Explores predictive analytics and its role in decision-making, a critical element in AI applications for project management.
17. Agrawal, A., Gans, J., & Goldfarb, A. (2018). Prediction Machines: The Simple Economics of Artificial Intelligence. Harvard Business Review Press.
    - Focuses on AI as a tool for better predictions in various domains, including project management.
18. Sinek, S. (2009). Start with Why: How Great Leaders Inspire Everyone to Take Action. Portfolio.
    - While not directly related to AI, this book offers insights into leadership principles that AI can enhance.

Research Papers and Articles

19. Chui, M., Manyika, J., & Miremadi, M. (2016). Where Machines Could Replace Humans—and Where They Can't (Yet). McKinsey Quarterly.
    - Discusses areas where AI excels and its limitations, useful for identifying how it can enhance project management.
20. Ng, A. (2017). AI Transformation Playbook. Landing AI.
    - A step-by-step guide to implementing AI solutions in business processes.
21. Ford, M. (2021). The Impact of Automation on Project

Management: A Case Study. Journal of Business Studies Quarterly.

- Examines how automation driven by AI can reshape project workflows.

Web Resources

22. AI in Project Management Blog – AI-Powered Project Solutions
    - A dedicated blog offering real-world examples and tutorials for integrating AI into project management.
    - https://ai-projectmanagement.com
23. AI Ethics Lab
    - A hub for exploring ethical considerations in AI applications, including their use in project management.
    - https://aiethicslab.com
24. MIT Technology Review – Artificial Intelligence Section
    - Regular updates on AI advancements and their applications across industries.
    - https://www.technologyreview.com

Tools and Platforms

25. ClickUp
    - A project management platform with AI-driven task prioritization and automation features.
    - https://www.clickup.com
26. Tableau
    - Advanced data analytics and visualization platform with AI-driven forecasting tools.
    - https://www.tableau.com

27. JIRA with Automation
    - A tool for agile project management with AI capabilities to streamline workflows.
    - https://www.atlassian.com/software/jira

Case Studies and Industry Reports

28. Accenture (2022). AI and Project Management: Driving Efficiency and Innovation.
    - Highlights success stories of AI implementations in various industries, including aerospace and cybersecurity.
    - https://www.accenture.com
29. Deloitte Insights (2023). AI Trends in Business 2023.
    - Covers how AI is being leveraged to improve operational efficiencies, including in project management.
    - https://www2.deloitte.com
30. PwC (2021). AI Predictions: How AI Will Shape the Future of Business.
    - Focuses on the future of AI applications and strategies for successful integration.
    - https://www.pwc.com

***